Parrots

Everything
About Purchase,
Care, Feeding, and
Housing

Filled with Full-color
Photographs

Illustrations by
Michele Earle-Bridges

BARRON'S

CONTENTS

THE COMPANION PARROT

No matter what they thought it would be, most people are surprised to see that life with a parrot is more—more entertaining, more complicated, more engaging—than they ever expected. A parrot can spark incredibly creative interplay with humans, other birds, and pets. They are always ready to astonish us with vocalizations that might be mimicked, used with association, or simply invented.

This book provides a practical approach to caring for companion parrots and to helping humans and birds adjust to each other's ways. Part of this involves selecting a bird with needs you know you can fulfill. Part of it involves tolerance and human willingness to accommodate an exuberant, determined individual with feathers, wings, and a beak.

Companion parrots, for they are considered more than pets, exude a contagious delight in simple things—toys, daylight, good clean water. A parrot might court you, solicit your every attention, serenade you with sweet love songs night and day for years, then jilt you for your spouse or mother-in-law. Or the bird might be absolutely terrified of something as innocuous as a new lamp, even though it wants to court a huge, live, bull mastiff! A parrot, even a small

The needs of every human and pet in the household must be considered before adding a parrot to the mix.

parrot, might suddenly decide that nobody except a favorite teenager is allowed in the kitchen.

Each bird is a unique individual, complete with complex social skills and self-directed motivations that may not seem particularly social. And, learning the skills needed to live harmoniously with a parrot can be just a little tricky. Unlike the carnivorous dogs and cats we are so used to, birds are prey species, whose ancestors survived by fleeing. They may have very different reactions to usually predictable household situations than a predatory pet would have.

Birds also have special safety needs that not everybody catches on to right away. They are endangered by some surprising hazards such as open standing water (toilets, hot tubs, fish tanks), windows, mirrors, and fumes from overheated Teflon cookware that didn't seem threatening before parrots lived indoors (see Hazards in the Home, page 26).

All About Feathers

Parrots can make their wants and needs known vocally, but we also learn a great deal about a parrot by looking at its feathers. Feathers might be bright, clean and shiny, generally an indication of good health and nutrition. Or they might be dull and broken, perhaps even chewed by the parrot itself.

With the exception of bare facial patches in macaws and African Greys, parrots are almost completely covered by assorted types of feathers—protein structures used for insulation, flight, communication, and protection. Down feathers are soft, plumed, usually gray or white feathers that grow next to the body. These are "underwear" feathers that are seldom seen while still attached to the bird, but appear suddenly on the floor when warm weather hits. Down feathers are covered by larger, smoother, protective feathers called contours. Tight,

slightly cupped, shell-shaped contour feathers cover the breast and back, while longer, harder feathers that facilitate flight and balance grow on wings and tail.

Body language: An observant human can pick up clues to a bird's behavior by observing its "body language." A bird with head bowed and neck feathers ruffled is usually asking for a scratch. A bird lifting a foot is probably asking to be picked up. A bird approaching skin with ruffled head feathers and an open beak is likely to bite whatever it is looking at.

Display: A parrot is never more beautiful than when it extends its shoulders and fans its tail feathers in "display." Colors and markings are vividly displayed. This beautiful exhibition is part of both courtship and defense of territory. Like human clothing, the display is used to attract mates. All feathers might be spread, with body and head feathers sticking straight out making the bird look much larger. In conflicts over mates and territory, this feather show usually takes the place of actual battle as one parrot drives the other away merely by showing how large and fierce it can look with all feathers fanned and beak open in threatened attack. A parrot in this pose may be considering mating or biting. In indoor settings where the bird does not have the option to stay or fly away, fanned feathers and an open beak could be more than a threat.

"Emotions": A parrot uses its feathers to express fear (smooth feathers, leaning backward), longing (leaning forward,

1. down (under) feather
2. contour (body-covering feather
3. flight (wing) feather

wings spread slightly, quivering), happiness (fluffy head feathers), or transition (tail wag). The way feathers are held might also indicate well-being, with a healthy bird expressing emotions using many different postures to express many different moods. A parrot that is not feeling well might show little interest in toys or interaction or might sit listlessly with body feathers puffed out for warmth. A parrot might chew its own feathers as a response to the stress of boredom, or it might develop feather chewing as a habit as humans develop habitual nail biting.

Molting

Like human eyelashes, parrot feathers do not continually lengthen, but rather grow to maturity, then remain exactly the same size and shape until they fall out. A new feather cannot grow in until the old feather falls out. This process is called *molting*. Old feathers fall out in mirror image pairs on opposite sides of the body so that the functions of flight and body covering are not affected. Young, active birds might replace every feather every year. Larger, older, sedentary birds may molt less completely, replacing all feathers in two- or three-year cycles .

Some parrots molt almost continuously, but most parrots molt after the season for reproducing during the time in which young would fledge—usually during warm weather. Down feathers are usually shed first. By June, in the United States, there will be daily accumulations of feathers to be vacuumed. New parrot owners are often surprised to see accumulations of shed feathers during almost any warm snap or anytime the ambient temperature increases by 10°F or more.

The Case of the Creative Parrot

Cosmo, a Green-cheeked Amazon, has a modest vocabulary of human words used with understanding. As with most companion parrots, the meanings of the words are Cosmo-assigned associations—simple, creative, understandable. The word "cracker" isn't just crackers, but rather crackers and almost any other yummy, nut- or seed-like food.

Being an Amazon, of course, Cosmo is well acquainted with water, knows and uses the word "water." The meaning here, traditionally Amazonian, is *"Wow, wonderful wet stuff!"*

The first time he was given a grape, when beak broke through fleshy skin, Cosmo was squirted in the face. Eyeballing the unfamiliar goody with both hard and wet properties, he christened it "crack water." After that, Cosmo's vocabulary included "crack water" for grapes, based on its dual characteristics, as well as "crackers" and "water" for their previous meanings.

Cosmo is a smart bird, but then, he lived with a very smart man. Cosmo's guardian was Robert Olen Butler who won the Pulitzer Prize for writing "Mr. Green," a story about women and religion that looks and sounds like a parrot story. This incident was reported in an interview with Robert Olen Butler regarding his book *Good Scent from a Strange Mountain*.

Allopreening

New feathers that still retain a blood supply, grow out from the skin enclosed in sheaths of protein similar to fingernail cuticle. The sheath gradually dries out and flakes off as the feather opens from the tip. This cover is removed during preening. But a parrot can't reach its own head

A young companion parrot should be fully weaned and learn to fly before moving to its first home.

Disparate size can be hazardous, even fatal, to a smaller bird.

A bowed head and ruffled neck feathers invite a scratch.

A well-adjusted macaw enjoys both face to face interactions and independent activities.

or neck. By late summer, a bird that doesn't have companions might have little spikes on its head and neck that look like toothpicks that have been dipped in glue. A human or bird companion might help the bird to get these feather sheaths off, a process called *allopreening*, but many high-strung parrots won't allow this kind of touching. Increasing showers from twice weekly to every day will help feather sheaths naturally break up and flake away.

The Way of the Beak

A parrot's beak is hard and can be sharp and painful if used against skin. It functions as a hand, a nutcracker, a grooming device, and a courtship tool, among other things. The beak might be used in an aggressive way to encourage a too-aggressive human to leave it alone or to let one know that a particular interaction is unacceptable to the bird. Companion parrots—who have no recourse to flee—will resort to biting when frightened. This is a natural reaction called the "fight-or-flight" response. A fear bite is the most painful bite of all.

Baby companion parrots also use their beaks in peaceful ways. Parrots love to groom or preen beards or the hair on favorite humans. Unfortunately, they also want to remove anything "foreign" on skin, and this might include moles. This is merely grooming with no intent to cause pain. A parrot that wants to be picked up might grab at a human walking by or will gently pull a hand closer in order to step up.

Bacon and Pork Chop, the famous potbellied pigs, with the Vincents, their dog, and Einstein, Crackers, and Comet—stars of the Thunderbirds flying bird show.

Flashing eyes and many ruffled feathers may signal aggression.

Many parrots will want to groom human teeth. This must not be allowed, of course, for human saliva contains organisms harmful to birds.

Humans must learn to use their hands appropriately to stimulate and reinforce only peaceful uses of the beak. When petting the beak or the skin around the beak, always have the thumb and index finger situated to the

More Than Pigs?

John and Lynn Vincent have five house pigs, several outdoor pigs, a goat or two, a donkey, a couple of Clydesdales, and a European wild boar. Otherwise they might be any other young couple, both aerospace engineers, who own a famous potbellied pig show.

It came as no surprise when they announced that they were expanding their show to include a blue-and-gold macaw. The bird was small for its species, a bird selected with a natural predisposition for flying. It was guaranteed already trained to fly to humans when prompted. And it did.

I visited them the first day the bird was in the home and was amazed at the baby bird that loved to fly to people and at how very, very clean a home with five pigs could be. The house was simply spotless, carpeted throughout because pigs don't like to walk on hard, slick floors.

A few days later, I had a call from an amazed new macaw owner. It was Lynn.

"Do you know how many animals we have?"

"Yes, I think so," I replied, thinking of Top Hog, the boar with a coat like a hairbrush.

"Well, we clean up a lot of poop here, and we're amazed that, considering its size, this bird seems to poop more than any other animal!"

It obviously wasn't much of an issue. Now, the Vincents have Comet, a greenwing macaw, and Einstein, an African Grey.

The parrot's chewing habits are legend. If the companion bird has enough things to chew, the beak gradually wears away to a length and configuration typical of each species. In nature, most hookbills are cavity breeders, that is, they hollow out tree trunks to make their nests. In our homes, their need to chew can seem voracious. A bird with nothing to chew could be called an abused bird. Appropriate and diverse chewable elements of the environment such as perches and toys provide chewing opportunities. A busy, self-reliant bird has happy humans.

Birds' Poop

Healthy parrots are very clean creatures. They bathe frequently, preen or groom daily, and do not tolerate dirty plumage, beaks, or feet. However, almost all birds are famously untidy about their surroundings. Combine the debris that comes from chewing wood, paper, fabric, and leather toys, with partially eaten food, molted feathers, and droppings, and there is potential for quite a mess. More than one bird has lost its home because humans were unprepared or poorly prepared for the natural clutter that accompanies parrots.

Remember, what goes in must come out, and the smaller the bird, the smaller the droppings. Management of droppings may be crucial to the bird's acceptance by every individual human in the home. Selecting a smaller bird is sometimes recommended if anyone in the family is especially sensitive about tidiness.

Well-designed equipment can make or break a parrot's chances for acceptance in a human environment. Look for labor- and time-saving features to deal with various aspects of bird care and cleaning. They are often well worth

opposite sides of the beak so that if the bird opens and closes its beak, the digits are pushed apart, rather than one winding up in the beak.

the investment, but tolerance for a little mess may be the most necessary component for a long, happy life with a parrot.

Expectations

While we can expect a little mess, few other aspects of living with a parrot are absolutely predictable, and therein lies both the greatest potential for joy and the greatest potential for aggravation. Just as every human child is a source of surprise and wonder for loving and appreciative adults, every bird brings its own surprise and wonder, even in homes that have many, many birds.

Companion parrots express themselves with words, song, and postures, sometimes including aggression. Some birds will express their wants, needs, and "emotions" in ways that most humans appreciate. Each may respond differently to a given situation, and some responses may be problematic. Even vocalizations can become an issue, as a parrot might learn to use words its humans don't want to hear. Some of the "songs" sung in parrot language may not be pleasing to human ears. Additionally, if a parrot is capable of repeating human words and song, it will almost surely want to sound like humans in other ways. That means coughs, sneezes, belches, heavy breathing, and worse. And they may use these very human sounds at just those times when humans least expect them and least want to hear them.

A parrot's instinctual motivation is to reproduce. Territorial responses by mature birds probably seem temperamental when described in human terms. If cooperation is not established as a part of the bird's routine responses, then the bird may become increasingly self-motivated and less cooperative as time passes, even in the most hospitable and well-meaning home. Routine cooperation exercises (see page 39) also serve to establish confidence in these naturally cautious creatures.

Don't be surprised to see fear reactions, however, even in a well-adjusted bird. Because parrots are genetically programmed to flee danger and cannot flee when confined, fear can complicate almost any already existing issue. Companion parrots must be protected from both long-term and short-term complications of fear responses. A healthy, active bird can get into trouble quickly. We must be ready for anything, anytime.

LOOKING FOR JUST THE RIGHT BIRD

The notion of sharing life with a parrot comes to each person differently. Some are thunderstruck when they meet a bird in a friend's home. Some fall in love with a bird that just happens to be looking for someone to fall in love with.

Breeders and Dealers

When you're dreaming of adding a feathered companion to your life, be careful where you go, and don't take your checkbook or credit cards when you know you're going to see darling baby birds. Expect to visit a bird you're considering several times before actually taking it home. An impulse decision can be bad both for you and for the bird.

A dependable source will be concerned about your motivations and intentions toward the bird. A premium hand-fed baby parrot represents many hours, possibly years, of feeding, cleaning, and socialization. When you ask questions about the dealer's practices and expertise, expect to be questioned about your own practices and expertise. Many breeders, dealers, stores, and adoption organizations will

A parrot is a bird with a hard, hooked upper beak, a mallet-shaped tongue, and four toes, two opposing two.

expect you to have read this book or other books about parrots, perhaps even requiring multiple visits to the bird and classroom training before taking one of their babies home.

Since 1993 all baby parrots available as human companions in the United States have been hatched in the United States. But even indoors, some parrots reproduce seasonally, and certain species might hatch in great numbers, creating a surplus of that species in a particular area at a particular time. It is only natural for a breeder or dealer to have a strong desire to place a bird that is available *now*. For this reason, many thoughtful breeders maintain a waiting list so that they can provide exactly as many parrots as homes available.

A responsible breeder or dealer will give some sort of written guarantee of the bird's health and condition. Any early veterinary care should be disclosed, whether that care was for illness, well-bird examination, DNA sexing, or microchip implanting. A guarantee might include a well-baby checkup by an avian veterinarian and would probably pay for treatment or replacement if an illness was present at the time the bird went to the new home.

▬▬ CHECKLIST ▬▬

Shopper's Etiquette
✔ When looking for a parrot, be sure to visit only one breeder or dealer daily.
✔ Bathe, change clothing, and shoes before visiting each facility. Baby parrots don't have fully formed immune systems. Expect to be required to wash your hands before handling babies.
✔ Be sure to ask permission to handle birds as some dealers allow babies to be handled only with supervision. This protects the baby (and the interests of their future families) from handling mishaps.
✔ Interact, hold, and touch babies gently and carefully.
✔ Don't provoke the birds by pointing or waving fingers in their faces.
✔ Don't encourage flapping if the baby has food in the crop, as it might aspirate formula into the air sacs.
✔ Don't tease or allow children to tease the birds. Waving a hand, for example, might either frighten or provoke a sensitive parrot. Especially don't let anybody pull or touch a parrot's tail. Even a simple touch on the tail can make a parrot nervous, as a bird in the wild with a touched tail is probably a dead bird.

What Are Your Choices?

While a parrot is, indeed, a parrot, there are lots of differences between available types. (Expected traits of common varieties of companion parrots are described in Barron's, *Guide to Companion Parrot Behavior* by Mattie Sue Athan.) And, there can be extreme variations between individuals of the same type. Generally, a smaller bird can be expected to develop less invasive habits, but this is not always true. Some of the small parrots can have extremely "big" voices. For example, both Amazons and full-sized macaws have loud voices, but Amazons are more likely to use them frequently. Mini macaws more resemble Amazons in the frequency and loudness of their calls.

It is also impossible to predict exactly how each different household member will react to the addition of a parrot. However, by interviewing people who live with parrots, people who breed parrots, people who deal with parrot behavior problems, and people who find second homes for parrots, it is possible to predict common issues.

The chart on page 18 is *not* a rating of the birds. The Potential Issues Index is an estimate of the frequency and importance of common factors affecting homes where humans live with parrots. These are *potential* issues, of course, and not every situation achieves the same potential. Each column represents an aspect of companion parrot reality such as how much space each bird needs, how much mess humans can tolerate, how often humans are intolerant of parrot sounds, reactions to the bird's attention needs, and the ability of humans to tolerate beak on flesh. Each issue is then rated according to how often these factors affect the ability of each type of bird to keep its home. Please note that a rating of 0 does not mean that the bird has zero needs in the category, but rather that the bird's needs are considered minimal.

Be careful—a mismatch between humans and bird has the potential to adversely affect the bird more than the humans.

Age of the Bird

Once there is some idea of what species of bird to look for, we must also consider the age of the bird:

• An unweaned bird. Although the baby must remain with the hand-feeder at least until it eats independently and is acclimated to the cage, many people prefer to place a deposit on an unweaned bird. Visiting during hand-feeding greatly reduces the amount of stress the young-ster experiences when it goes to the new home. The bird needs the strength and confidence that comes with flying. Fledging also facilitates the development of balance and coordination and may prevent feather damaging behaviors or other unintended consequences in the future. Modestly trim the wings at least until the first molt so that humans can learn to accommodate bird safety issues (see Safety First: Grooming the Indoor Bird, page 19).

• A newly weaned baby (presuming that the bird has already learned to fly). For many years, this was considered ideal. Many breeders now keep their babies, when possible, until they have flown for at least a few weeks.

• A 9–24-month-old bird. While many breeders and dealers don't like to keep babies this long, these can be some of the best finds. The bird may have already worked through develop-mental phases that could have proved difficult in a solitary setting with inexperienced

The Case of the Matching Cockatoo

Forrest, an antiques dealer, loses his canary to old age. Browsing the bird store for a replacement, he happens upon a totally charming off-white parrot just the beige peach color of his antique fainting couch. Selecting a lovely domed cage 24 inches (62 cm) in diameter, he takes his new Goffin's cockatoo (Cacatua goffini) home to his small but lavishly furnished condominium.

There's a clash coming between antiques and beak and between human and parrot needs. A Goffin's cockatoo will scream non-stop or absolutely self-destruct when kept in such a small cage, and it will chew a great deal of antique wood if it is not confined. The bird lasts less than three months in its first disastrous home.

humans, and the immune system will be fully formed, minimizing the possibility of health issues. It is easier to see a bird's inherent per-sonality at this age than when it's younger.

• An older, secondhand parrot. This can be an excellent choice, but it can also be problematic if health or behavioral issues were not previ-ously addressed. On the other hand, a second-hand parrot might be a matter of inheritance, necessity, or charity that doesn't really involve a decision. See Barron's *The Second-hand Parrot* by Mattie Sue Athan and Dianalee Deter for further information on this subject.

Selecting a Particular Bird

✔ Look for an alert, hearty, curious bird. The chick should be plump and active; eyes should be shining, interested. The beak should be

symmetrical, with clear, dry nostrils. Feet should open and close and should be well situated under the chick. Check for four toes on each foot, with toenails on each toe. One or two missing toes or toenails won't affect adjustment. Multiple missing toes or toenails might require special accommodation.

✔ Avoid extremely shy or actively fearful chicks. Babies showing noticeable aggression or noticeable fear should be avoided until these issues have been resolved.

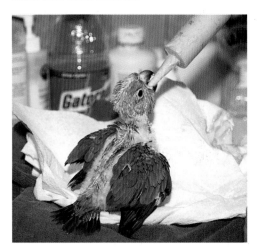

Baby parrots learn to play even before they are mature enough to fly or eat independently.

✔ Don't be overly concerned about less-than-perfect feathers. Young birds may have ratty-looking feathers until they learn to preen, but be wary of a bird with multiple stress bars or damage lines straight across the feathers that may indicate health or nutritional issues.

✔ Droppings should be well formed, with three observable parts, feces (solid material), urates (chalky white material), and liquid (clear fluid). Runny droppings might indicate a health issue or might mean that the bird has just eaten fruit. Veterinary examination is necessary to confirm the bird's condition.

✔ If talking is important, look for a bird that is already talking. Even some unweaned baby parrots may have acquired a few human words. Look for a vocally experimental bird that is willing to make sounds, even baby sounds, in your presence.

✔ Now that gender can be safely and easily determined with inexpensive DNA analysis, many parrot breeders and dealers have their babies sexed before selling them. If you want a bolder bird you should look for a bolder chick without regard to gender, for although most hens do seem to be more cautious, we see many very gregarious, outgoing hens, even some who went through a shy phase or phases. We also see territorial hens and shy cocks.

✔ Look for a dealer who is sensitive to the bird's needs during the weaning process. The presence of other birds, including other babies, can be important. While the babies are weaning, they

NEONATE: an unweaned baby parrot.

The weaned, fledged, baby companion parrot should have its wing feathers carefully trimmed before going to the new home.

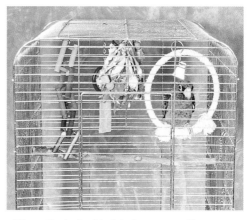

Allow the baby bird to become well acclimated to the cage before leaving the hand feeder.

rely on each other for support, encouragement, and a sense of security. They learn from each other how to play and how to get around in a cage, what to eat, what to chew, and what to fear.

Preparing for the First Big Move

Resist the temptation to suggest that weaning be hurried along. Forced weaning should be discouraged. Each individual bird should be allowed to give up hand-feeding in its own time and not be held to a schedule.

The Cage

Allow the bird to become well acclimated by moving into a transitional cage (see page 25), at least a week before leaving the

Birds that fly indoors encounter many safety issues.

hand-feeder. It is good to have other babies exploring and experiencing the cage there with your bird. Outfit the cage with toys and appropriate perches before taking everything home.

Just because the cage is the right size, don't assume that the perches will be right; every bird has different-sized feet, and the baby bird should be able to grip almost all of the perches, not just rest, open-footed, on top of

Potential Issues Index

**0 = not usually an issue, 1 = occasionally an issue, 2 = a common issue,
3 = can be an important issue, 4 = can be an extreme issue**

	Size/Space Needs	Mess/Care Tolerance	Sound Tolerance	Attention Needs	Bite Tolerance	Total
Budgie (Parakeet)	1	2	0	0	0	3
Cockatiel	1	1	1	1	0	4
Lovebird, Parrotlet	1	1	1	0	2	5
Quaker (Monk)	1	1	2	1	2	7
Small Poicephalus	1	1	2	1	2	7
Rosella, Grass Parakeet	2	1	2	0	2	7
Pionus	1	1	2	1	2	7
Ringneck	2–3	1–2	2–3	0	2	7–10*
Mini Macaw	1–2	2	2–4	1	2–3	8–12*
Conure, Brotegeris	1–2	1–2	3–4	1	2–3	8–12*
Cape	3	3	2	1	1	10
Caique	1	1	3	3	3	11
Lory	2	4	2–3	1–2	2–3	11–14
African Grey	2	2	3	3	3	13
Amazon	2	2	4	2	3	13
Eclectus	3	3	2	3	3	14
Macaw	4	4	3	2–3	3–4	16–18*
Cockatoo	3	4	4	4	4	19

1–5 Potential Issues are MINIMAL: These birds have minimal needs and modest related costs. Most individuals and families can adjust to these birds.

6–10 Potential Issues are AVERAGE: These birds usually have reasonable, easy-to-accommodate needs that can be provided in most homes. A few individuals or individual members of a family unit may be intolerant of these birds.

11–15 Potential Issues are GREAT: These birds can be accommodated in well-balanced families or by solitary individuals who know themselves to be tolerant and amenable. More than a few humans may be unable to adjust to these birds.

16–20 Potential Issues are EXTREME: These birds require many accommodations and are suited to individuals who are generous, consistent, and tolerant. A majority of people may be unable to provide adequately for or adjust to these birds.

*Extreme size and other variations in these birds result in a greater range of issues.

the perch. Don't make a sensitive baby parrot sleep on a concrete perch.

Diet

The new bird should have to endure as few changes as possible in the transition to the permanent home; the diet, especially, should remain the same in the new home. The bird should have been weaned onto a healthy diet. It should receive a similar nutritious variety of interesting foods as it enjoyed while weaning. If a diet change is necessary, it should be done well after the bird is comfortable in the new home.

Safety First: Grooming the Indoor Bird

While it's important to allow a baby bird to fly before bringing it home, a good wing trim and careful transportation procedures are necessary to protect a new parrot from the unfamiliar dangers in the new home. Always transport your bird in a hard-sided carrier, a necessary piece of equipment for ensuring its safety in a moving vehicle.

Trimming Wing Feathers

Flight becomes a safety issue in indoor habitats where common human objects and activities can be dangerous to birds. Serious, even fatal, accidents can occur in seconds. Veterinarians and behavior consultants in the United States have long observed that companion parrots live longer and experience fewer accidents if their wing feathers are kept

TIP

Wing Trims

✔ A very minimal, noninvasive trim must be frequently maintained, as the bird can regain flight with only one long new feather.

✔ Don't expect to take your bird outdoors without a cage. Even a severely trimmed pudgy Amazon can be blown away on a very windy day.

✔ If a companion bird's wing feathers are untrimmed, it must be trained to fly dependably to humans upon request. Only harnessed birds should be allowed outdoors without a cage or carrier.

✔ If your bird flies away, go after it (see page 83). It's the right thing to do.

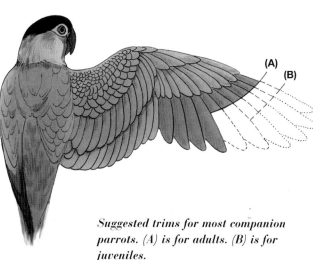

(A)
(B)

Suggested trims for most companion parrots. (A) is for adults. (B) is for juveniles.

A carrier is necessary to safely transport the new baby parrot.

trimmed. Most people probably have their birds' wing feathers trimmed at least twice yearly.

Like all feathers, wing feathers grow out only after they are shed. They are best trimmed symmetrically, so that birds retain balance and confidence. Birds groomed in this way are happy and seldom develop related behavioral issues.

Use the least invasive trim necessary. Feathers are trimmed enough to restrict, but not completely prevent, flight. This is beneficial and compassionate. Only primary flight feathers are modified, for only primaries enable altitude; other wing feathers are for protection, maneuverability, or braking. Never forget that even radically trimmed birds can be blown away by a gust of wind. A companion parrot, trimmed or untrimmed, should not go outdoors without a cage or harness.

Each bird's grooming configuration must be suited to its disposition. After a few visits and a little training, a careful owner can usually learn to maintain wings. This might be suggested in bold, not shy, companion parrots. Happy interactions with towels are essential to success here (see The Towel Game, page 41).

A professional groomer or veterinarian will usually know what a particular bird needs. Be sure to let the groomer know exactly what you want done *before* feathers are trimmed. (Refer to Barron's *Guide to Companion Parrot Behavior* by Mattie Sue Athan for suggested wing trims specific to the particular type of bird, the bird's age, and flight ability.)

A typical trim for a young parrot might begin with only half of the first three feathers from the outside as they are seen from the top. This will keep a curious young bird from smashing hard into a window, but should not affect the bird enough to keep it from enjoying the sensation of flapping. As the bird develops additional muscle tone, balance, and expertise, three to five—seven in the case of budgies, cockatiels, and other small parrots with long feathers—additional feathers may be trimmed back halfway or a little more. It is easier on the bird if too little is trimmed rather than too much.

A good wing trim is recoverable. Be careful. If too many feathers are trimmed too short or if they are trimmed shorter than the layer of feathers protecting their bases (the coverts), they might regrow with difficulty or even be unable to replace themselves again.

A few parrots are bothered by cut edges of feathers, and some veterinarians prefer to clip these birds' feathers under the coverts. If the veterinarian or groomer *insists* that wing feathers be trimmed shorter than the coverts, don't allow more than four (the outside) flight feathers to be cut. Fewer cut feathers are easier to regrow than more cut feathers.

Toenails

Baby birds should be allowed to have sharp toenails (so that they won't fall), but an adult parrot's nails should not raise the ball under the end of the toe up off a flat surface. Tiny little human nail clippers may be used on small birds. For birds the size of a Quaker or larger, grind toenails with a cordless Dremel, a tool used for this purpose. Heat produced by the grinding stone cauterizes the blood supply, minimizing the risk of bleeding. If bleeding is experienced during nail grooming, it can be stopped with Qwik-stop styptic powder.

Beak

Most companion parrots require little or no beak maintenance. Beak deformities are rare, but sometimes worsen with growth and require reshaping. The beak is extremely sensitive, so any beak grooming, if necessary, should be done only by a professional. A Dremel should never be used on the beak of small birds because the vibration of the tool could injure or kill the bird. Occasionally, very cooperative parrots allow and actually enjoy gentle beak and nail filing with an emery board during towel play.

The Guarantee and the Well-Baby Checkup

While many breeders or dealers give a written guarantee, not all of those written guaran-tees include a well-baby checkup by an avian veterinarian. The new bird should be taken to the veterinarian almost immediately, even if it appears perfect in every way. This facilitates the guarantee with professional verification of the bird's condition.

Look for an experienced, board-certified avian veterinarian or at least one who is a member of the Association of Avian Veterinarians. If the bird came with a free or prepaid exam from a qualified avian veterinarian, by all means take advantage of that free exam. However, if the veterinarian does not do tests, consider finding one who does.

Tests done at this time establish a record so that comparisons can be made in the future. The costs of diagnostic tests are not usually included in most guarantees. However, tests are well worth the investment of time and money if the bird is not as healthy as it appears. If the veterinarian finds a health problem, the guarantee should cover treatment or allow for the bird's return.

Schedule the veterinarian appointment as early in the day as possible. Take the bird in its cage or take the bird in a carrier and bring the papers from the bottom of the cage so that the veterinarian can assess the bird's droppings and what the bird has been eating from the morning's food debris.

The well-bird checkup also helps the new caretakers to develop a relationship with the veterinarian and to understand the protocol for taking a bird in for medical care. This one step of preconditioning can save the bird's life if there is an accident or illness later.

Just pretend for a moment that you have met a parrot that you like, and the bird is interviewing potential owners as though they were job applicants. Of course, no human is perfect, but just suppose a parrot could select the least imperfect human with whom it would go home. What kinds of concerns would a parrot have? If a parrot could choose, would it choose you?

✔ *Can you love me as a companion, not a pet?*

I'm not the adoring-ground-worshipping-no-matter-what-you-do pet a dog would be.

Expect me to have a personal agenda with individualistic motivations that might seem selfish and egocentric, such as those a human might have.

✔ *Can you make the personal sacrifices necessary to accommodate me?*

Some people don't like the idea of giving up Teflon cookware to protect a bird. Can you ban smoking in the rooms where I live? Can you wear earrings with backs that pop off so that I can't damage your ear if I try to grab an earring and run?

✔ *Will you buy good equipment for me?*

My cage home has to keep me safe, fed, and entertained. If it's too small, I'll hate it and I'll let you know it. If it's ugly, you'll hate it and banish it, and me in it, to the garage or basement. I could develop some very unpleasant responses to your responses to my cage.

✔ *Will you give me good food and clean water?*

If I don't have healthy food, I might do fine for a while, but I would gradually weaken and die. It might take a long time, but it will happen. Spoiled, moldy food or dirty water can make me cranky and noisy almost immediately.

✔ *Will you make it easy for me to bathe according to my own preference?*

We parrots need lots of moisture to keep feathers clean and supple and to help express energy we can't use flying, foraging, and finding and defending nest sites. Some birds like showers; some birds like to bathe in a bowl.

✔ *Will you protect me from danger and boredom?*

While some dogs, some children, and household items can be dangerous to parrots, even simple boredom can have life-threatening consequences.

Some parrots prefer showers.

Will you keep me in toys and chewables so that I won't wind up chewing on myself? Can you remember to keep the toilet lid down and the bathroom and outside doors closed to protect me from accidents.

✔ *Will you be able to forgive me if I bite you?*

I've got this can opener-like thing on the front of my face, and it's only natural that sometimes I might use it to get my way. You can't take it personally. How will you react if I bite?

✔ *Will you give me a proper education?*

You can teach me to bite by reinforcing bad behavior, and an abundance of bad behavior might mean I would spend my later years homeless or in a sanctuary. Can you keep from laughing if I bite somebody else? Can you guide me to learn correct behavior?

✔ *Will you keep my grooming up to date?*

It does neither of us any good if my nails are sharp and you react badly. My nails must be short enough not to hurt you or to get caught in things in my environment. And then there's the matter of flying: If my wing feathers aren't kept trimmed, I might accidentally fly away and not be able to find my way home. If I fly away, will you keep looking until you find me?

✔ *Will you take care of me if I get sick?*

If I look sick, I probably am, and veterinary care isn't free. It's not unusual to have to drive 50 miles or more to a respected avian veterinar-

Some parrots prefer bathing in shallow water, and some can be induced to bathe with ice cubes in the water.

ian. If I am injured or if I become ill, are you willing to commit your time and money to ensure that I am not in pain or danger of death?

✔ *Are you ready for a long-term relationship?*

Parrots make a mess, and I am no exception—and, if I'm lucky, I could live for a very long time. How much time, how many years will you commit to caring for me?

✔ *Will you make sure I have a good place to go when you can no longer care for me?*

And since I might outlive you, will you make sure I go to someone who wants me? Will you put me in your will as a possession or an heir?

Note: Concept contributed by Cathy Isbell.

THE TRANSITION TO THE NEW HOME

The new parrot will be quiet, perhaps even sedentary the first few days in a new home. This is a natural response. The bird will gradually overcome caution and be more exploratory, especially if it was encouraged to be gregarious and experimental during the weaning process.

Most of the surprises that come the first few days in the new home are the result of novice bird owners being unfamiliar with the ways of birds. For example, flying away is one of the most common complications that might occur.

A Bird's Cage Is Its Castle

The cage is the bird's retreat—a safe haven. There are toys to play with, perches to climb and chew, good food, and clean water. There are no surprises, no demands, and no threats.

The primary function of the cage is to ensure the bird's safety. A normal curious parrot can get into a surprising amount of trouble in a typical human home. Birds love to explore. Left unsupervised they are in danger.

The secondary function of the cage is to ensure the bird's happiness. Keeping a parrot in an unsuitable cage can lead to unwanted

Both the home and the parrot must be protected from each other.

behaviors, but problematic behavioral issues can develop especially easily if a companion parrot has no cage, at all—rather like a kid with no bedroom.

Feeling insecure in the cage, being unable to adequately exercise, or losing sleep because of cage placement are common stressers that can contribute to the development of excessive dependence on human attention, feather picking, screaming, apathy, or aggression. To stimulate the best possible behavior in the bird, try to find the best possible cage.

A good cage serves the needs of the caretaker, too. The more *you* like the cage, the more you will enjoy doing the chores required to maintain the bird.

A Comfortable Cage

Most parrots can come into the home and go directly into a large cage that will accommodate their needs for a lifetime, but some sensitive baby parrots get the best start in a smaller cage during the first days or weeks in the home. Almost any baby parrot can exhibit

Hazards in the Home

Curiosity combined with wings and the ability to fly can kill a companion parrot. Whether this involves a window, a ceiling fan, a toilet, or a frying pan, the accident would probably have been inaccessible if the bird had not been able to fly. But even wing trims aren't perfect insurance against in-home accidents, and even a bird that can't fly must be carefully protected from the consequences of curiosity; a newly flighted bird, especially, that is unaccustomed to flying must be carefully supervised indoors. Here is what to watch out for:

✔ Parrots are sometimes suffocated in closets, beds, afghans, and drawers, but water is probably the most common cause of death in the home. A bird that cannot breathe dies in seconds. Drowning can occur quickly in unlikely ways: a parrot might be found head down in a glass of water, or floating in an unattended sink, bucket, bathtub, or aquarium.

✔ Loose strings from afghans, sweaters, or towels or partially dismantled toys can trap and injure a curious parrot.

✔ Parrots with liberty in the home must be protected from access to electrical cords and lead weights in draperies.

✔ Unscreened or unguarded torchère floor lamps get so hot they can easily injure an unsuspecting bird trying to land.

✔ Fumes generated by almost any burning plastics or by overheated Teflon (polytetrafluroethylene) can kill a parrot. Fumes from household cleaners, room deodorizers, scented candles, and incense can easily affect the parrot's sensitive respiratory system.

✔ Kitchens are especially dangerous where open pans might contain hot oil or other cooking foods. Fireplaces and wood-burning stoves can tragically maim or kill a flighted indoor bird in seconds. A bird that flies into an uncovered duct can fall directly into a basement or ground floor furnace.

✔ Domestic cats can be a danger to smaller birds as can children, but the more common danger from already established household residents is from dogs or ferrets. While most dogs or cats do not even seem to notice larger parrots, a ferret will go for any bird, regardless of size.

✔ An even greater danger is from adults who might use nicotine, alcohol, or prescription drugs. It is important for parrots to be protected from accidentally consuming these very dangerous items.

poor adjustment to a first cage, but reactive species such as African Greys, Poicephalus, and some cockatoos are especially sensitive to issues related to early fear responses.

An inappropriate cage might be hard to climb, with too many vertical bars and not enough horizontal bars. Especially if perches are also too large, the bird might thrash, fall, and engage in multiple attention-demanding behaviors. It might revert back to wanting to be hand-fed; it might begin chewing feathers, calling excessively, or developing redundant aggressive or fearful behaviors. A young bird that is thrashing, falling, or crashing more than a foot to the bottom of the cage needs to be in a smaller cage, at least temporarily.

A smaller transitional cage can provide a sense of security for the new young bird and maneuverability to help the new bird handler. This smaller baby cage might be used as a roost cage or a travel cage later. Sometimes, the bird's perception of the cage can be manipulated by raising the grate, making the cage seem smaller. Simply use rope or self-locking cable ties to secure the grate or a homemade "false grate" to a higher group of horizontal bars. Once the bird is confidently utilizing the entire space available, the grate can be lowered. If it is difficult or impossible to raise the grate, some birds adjust successfully to your lowering the perches to near the bottom, then gradually raising them as coordination and confidence increase.

Cage Cover

A bird in a new environment may feel more secure with at least a partial cover on the cage all the time, maybe a towel hung over just one end of the cage. Dianalee Deter suggests that if the bird is very shy, cover the entire top of the cage with towels or other fabric hanging down 4 or 5 inches (10–13 cm) all the way around. The bird can go up into this shrouded sanctuary for privacy in much the same way it might go up into a tree. (Put the baby bird into the cage *after* this cover is in place.)

The Permanent Cage

Size: An appropriate permanent cage is the largest possible cage that can be comfortably accommodated in your personal living space. A parrot that is frequently out doesn't require a cage as large as one that is left in most of the time. A larger cage is absolutely necessary especially if the bird spends the entire work-day in the cage, or if it has to be locked up for vacations. Never expect a bird to live happily in a cage that is less than one and a half times deeper than its wingspan and at least two or three times as wide. For very large parrots, a few manufactured cage lines now offer the alternative of sections that can be added on.

Material: The cage should also be attractive. A good-looking cage is welcome in human-occupied spaces longer and more often. Bars should be steel, brass, chrome, or "powder" coated. Stainless steel is best for extremely large parrots such as full-sized macaws and some cockatoos. Colorful powder-coated cages stand up to mid-sized parrots.

Dishes, surfaces, and bars: There should be at least three dishes (for wet food, dry food, and water) that can be removed and replaced from outside the cage. All surfaces, inside and out, should be accessible so that the cage can be easily cleaned. The bars should be too thick for the bird to bend and too close together to get its head through. All spacing around dishes and doors should be too small to allow the bird to stick its head between.

Trays and grates: There should be a deep, removable tray and, preferably, a removable grate. Some birds like to forage, eat, or play in the bottom of the cage. A grate allows most droppings to fall through, thereby providing an area where the bird can play without becoming contaminated by feces or food debris. The bars of the grate should be as close together as the bars in the rest of the cage.

Mess catchers: Winglike mess catchers attached above the floor and near the bottom of the cage help to contain both the mess *and* the bird. Some modern cages feature rolls of tear-off paper to simplify cage cleaning.

Loose loops in crochet and lace can entrap tiny toes and injure or kill an unsupervised parrot.

Most modern cages are self-supporting units on wheels for easy access and maneuverability.

Doors: The door should be large and latch securely. Some parrots, especially cockatoos, are extremely adept escape artists. These birds

may require a locking device to defeat this behavior. Be sure that the key or combination is readily available in case of fire or other emergency.

Note: Be sure to avoid round cages with domed tops that may have bar spacing that gets progressively narrower toward the top; this dangerous configuration can trap and injure parrot toes. An arched-top rectangular cage with two flat sides is my favorite, providing a little more inside space than a flat-topped cage; it also still has "corners."

Cage Placement

A baby parrot needs a stimulating environment, but the cage must be located in a place that fosters a sense of security, preferably in a corner, or with at least one side to a wall. The cage is best situated across from rather than beside a window. It should not be placed beside an open door that people and other animals typically rush through unannounced, as a figure suddenly appearing out of nowhere can be frightening to anybody.

The curious young bird will want to put everything into its beak and that can be hazardous both to the bird and to the beak. Be sure the cage is well separated from human knickknacks, art, and other paraphernalia.

Screaming bouts can appear in over-stimulated parrots who get too little sleep.

An appropriate cage is attractive, spacious, easy to clean, and easy to climb.

Perches and Toys

A perch is more than a place to sit; it is a toy that the bird can sit on. Chewable, destructible perches provide entertainment and exercise as well as keeping the feet and beak in good condition. Perches and toys are a form of perishable goods that will be regularly replaced. Perches that are too hard for the bird that is sitting on them to peel or chew up promote boredom and sedentary behavior. Generally speaking, smaller parrots usually do better on softer woods, and larger parrots do better on harder woods.

Perches made from tree limbs retaining their bark are best for the bird's feet. Dowels, branches that no longer have bark, and very hard wood, such as manzanita, may be too smooth to be easily gripped. If the parrot falls from its perch because it can't hold onto it, it

Toys are not optional for companion parrots.

may become discouraged from activity and even develop fearfulness as a part of its personality.

Crabapple, plum, and peach trees supply excellent perch material. Also, soft woods such as ailanthus and the birch family not only provide a good perching surface, but also provide

The Roost Cage

Screaming bouts can appear in parrots that are overstimulated and have had too little sleep—like children at a community picnic. They become increasingly hyperactive, insistent, and irritable as they become more exhausted. Humans do very well on seven or eight hours of sleep, but parrots are so recently from the jungle that they do best with ten to twelve hours of sleep.

Many parrots, especially cockatoos, let their people know, in no uncertain terms, when it's time for bed, but that parrot bedtime might be 7:30 P.M., far too early for most humans to want to retire. This is where the roost cage comes in. This cage need not be large or fancy; it is merely a quiet place to sleep away from the hustle and bustle of human activities. It might have been the baby cage, or it might also be used as a travel cage for vacations, transportation to the veterinarian, or other outings.

The roost cage is best situated in a room well away from the sights, sounds, and other stimulation in the human activity areas where the bird's regular cage and play area are located. The bird can go to bed earlier than humans so that it gets as much sleep as necessary. In homes with very long daytime cycles, such as those where humans rise well before sunrise and continue activity late at night, the bird might also enjoy short naps there throughout the day. Humans enjoy the quiet of the bird's sleeping time and the birds enjoy the benefit of the rest. If the roost cage is to be used with naps, it is best to use a human termination stimulus, an alarm clock or timer, to tell us when it is time to end the bird's nap.

entertainment as the birds strip off the bark. Once the bark is gone, the perch should be replaced.

Avoid perches that are too rough. Some, but not all parrots, tolerate an abrasive cement nail grooming perch, but this should be in front of the water bowl, not high in the cage. While these stone perches may help to wear down toenails, they also wear down the skin on the bottoms of the feet and can cause irritations, especially if the bird sleeps on only one foot. Don't use sandpaper-covered perches for this same reason.

The texture of bark on the perch will keep the beak in good condition as well as the feet. The parrot should have plenty of textures to chew, such as vegetable-tanned leather, wood, paper, cardboard, rope, and cloth. A few of the toys can be permanent and indestructible, but there should always be a variety of destructible toys.

Moving toys within the cage and regularly rotating or changing toys helps keep the parrot interested. Toys that are no longer played with can be put away for a few weeks, then, when reintroduced they are "new" again. Leftovers from old toys can be combined to make new toys.

Keep an eye on new toys to make sure they are not dangerous to the bird. Openings should either be too small for the bird's head to fit through or large enough for the whole body to fit through. Keep strings trimmed short so that toes don't get caught. Remove any metal items that the bird has managed to bend or break. Typically, the most dangerous part of the toy is the fastener that connects the toy to the cage. If the bird can open them or unhook them, it is possible that the fastener can get caught on the parrot's beak.

Encourage your parrot to play with toys by providing praise and attention when it is beating up a bell or shredding wood. Play with toys while holding the bird to demonstrate that this is acceptable and entertaining behavior. Encouraging independent play early on can go a long way toward keeping unwanted behaviors from developing.

What Parrots Eat

Baby birds should go to their first homes at least a week or two after they have been eating independently. The little parrot will have more confidence in its ability to meet its own needs and will be less frightened when the first caregiver and its baby flock disappear.

If a newly weaned bird discontinues eating on its own, take it immediately back to the breeder or dealer. It is not unusual for a baby bird to be so unsettled by the sudden changes that it "forgets" how to feed itself. The stress is simply too much. This is especially noteworthy regarding baby cockatiels. Once the bird gets back to familiar surroundings, it will remember again, and will be ready for the new home after just a little more time. If returning the bird isn't possible, call the veterinarian immediately. DO NOT presume that the baby bird will start eating if it is hungry enough. Parrots are so social that a newly isolated young bird can starve to death if allowed to do so. Again, weighing can verify the bird's condition.

An experienced avian veterinarian will be able to tell if a bird still needs hand-feeding, as well as if an illness is present. The veterinarian will also be able to give instructions on how to hand-feed, if that is necessary.

A bird's disposition as well as its health can suffer if the balance of the diet is thrown off in any direction. Parrots are omnivores; they naturally consume both vegetable and animal-sourced foods, but either too much meat or too many vegetables can have health consequences over the long term. That is important because so many parrots have the potential to live so many years. Obesity is not uncommon in birds that do not fly or at least flap vigorously every day. While it is cute in a chicken, a part of the human food chain, carrying too much weight can be life-threatening in a parrot.

Pellet-Based Diet and Table Food

The easiest way to provide good nutrition is by feeding a pellet-based diet and supplementing with vegetables and fruits and healthy table food. Sweet potatoes, squash, pumpkin, beets, mangoes, papaya, broccoli, carrots, peas, green beans, radishes, melons, red peppers, hot peppers, leaf lettuce, and tomatoes are a few examples of healthy vegetables and fruits.

Note: *Don't kiss a parrot beak to lips; especially, don't kiss a parrot that has just eaten a hot pepper!)*

Other healthy table food includes small amounts of lean meat, pasta, rice, beans, whole grain bread, and eggs. Dairy products such as yogurt and cheese can supply extra calcium, but birds do not digest these easily. Dairy should be given only occasionally and in small amounts.

Warning: DO NOT offer avocado or chocolate as either can be toxic. Foods that are high in fat, salt, caffeine, sugar, artificial flavors, and artificial colors should be avoided. Potato chips, French fries, ice cream, soda pop, candy, cake, cookies, and other junk foods can make a bird both fat and malnourished.

Healthy foods will help to ensure your bird's long life.

Food puzzles simulate the wild activity of foraging for food.

A well-bonded parrot might solicit food, toys, or attention.

A balanced diet: The balanced diet should probably resemble the human food pyramid, but significantly more research is required to ensure proper nutrition for each type of parrot and each individual bird. The greater variety of nutritional sources that are offered, the more likely that the bird's nutritional needs will be met.

Malnutrition is considered the most common dietary issue in companion parrots. In parrots, as in humans, malnutrition can coexist with obesity. Overeating or selectively overeating certain elements in the diet can easily lead to

Larger parrots who chew through destructible toys benefit from having a few, but not all, indestructible toys.

obesity. Because of its high oil content, seed is a common culprit here. A careful, meticulous person may be able to get away with feeding seed instead of pellets as long as the seed is fresh and supplemented with lots of other fresh foods. Seed is best offered sprouted, and sprouts have to be fresh.

Begging

Parrots often beg for or try to steal whatever the people around them are eating—they flatten themselves, lean toward the food, and quiver. This is natural for the bird, since eating is a "flock" behavior. Encouraging this behavior makes introducing new foods much easier and helps the bird feel like part of the family. A companion parrot may, within reason, eat healthy human food, but don't forget that one piece of pizza 1 inch (2.5 cm) square might contain more salt, oil, and calories than the bird should eat in a whole day. Cheese is difficult for parrots to digest and should be fed only in very small quantities. Huge, human-sized treats of anything, whether it's pizza or popcorn, can destroy the nutritional balance of a good parrot diet.

Weighing the Bird

An occasional complication in the new home is discontinuance of independent eating. Weighing the bird every day at the same time, preferably before it eats in the morning, safeguards against problems related to failure to eat as well as other health issues. Small weight fluctuations of 5 or 10 grams are not dangerous, but if the bird loses more than 10 to 20 percent of what it weighed when it came home, it may be in trouble.

Old Habits and New Foods

It is only natural for any well-meaning parrot caretaker to want the best for his or her bird. This does not mean that if the bird has huge quantities of food to choose from, it will be well nourished. Most parrots will pick out their favorite foods and eat nothing else. This is probably like giving a child a four-course,

balanced meal all at once and watching her eat only the French fries.

Variety

Variety is the best way to ensure complete nutrition. Limit amounts fed so that the bird is not full before all the food offered is consumed. More food can be given if the bird is still hungry. Low-calorie snacks such as celery, carrots, broccoli, and leaf lettuce can be left in the cage for the bird to munch on between meals.

Feeding soft foods, such as fruits, vegetables, cooked beans, and cooked rice at a different time than seeds or pellets is another way to encourage the parrot to eat a larger variety. Offer the soft food when the unfinished portion can be removed before it spoils. Alternatively, offer an amount that will be finished so that there will be none left to spoil.

Parrots often fear the unfamiliar. This generally includes new food. It is easy to fall into the trap of feeding the bird only what it likes to eat because introducing something new can be difficult and frustrating. However, once the bird gets used to eating a little of everything—except chocolate and avocado—it will readily experiment with unfamiliar food. (If it's in the bowl, I guess I should eat it!) And the bird will show health and attitude improvements as a result of a varied diet.

Modeling Eating Behavior

Eating is one of the behaviors that can be easily demonstrated for a parrot.
✔ Eat healthy food in front of the bird.
✔ Make a big, noisy deal out of enjoying it.
✔ Praise yourself for eating it.
✔ Offer some to your bird. If he isn't immediately interested, take it back and focus your attention

Potential Life Spans of Common Companion Parrots

Budgie	6–15
Lory	8–25
Lovebird, Parrotlet, Brotegeris	10–20
Cockatiel, Grass Parakeet	10–25
Conure, Quaker, Ringneck, Rosella	15–35
Poicephalus, Pionus, Caique	15–30+
Eclectus	20–30+
Mini Macaw	20–35+
African Grey	20–40+
Amazon	25–80+
Macaw	40–80+
Cockatoo	30–80+

on the food. Feed it to another parrot or person or pet. Let them make a big deal out of it as well. Eventually, your bird will want to see what all the fuss is about and will try the food.

Parrots function on something like two-year-old-human "logic," that if "somebody else has something, it must be worth getting. Putting unfamiliar food on the human plate automatically classifies the food as "forbidden fruit," and therefore worthy of being stolen. Your bird wants to try it just because he saw it with the food being consumed by the rest of the flock.

Hiding New Food

Hiding new food can also be effective; it simulates foraging behaviors that wild parrots would use. This is particularly useful if the bird prefers seed to vegetables. Mixing seed and vegetables into a cooked bread or egg mixture can trick the bird into eating it while trying to pick out the seeds. Mince or puree the new food and mix it into the dough or batter. Gradually the amount of seeds can be reduced as the amount and sizes of vegetables are increased.

A boring diet can lead to behavior problems as well as ill health. Teaching the new companion parrot to enjoy a varied diet can be enjoyable, encouraging friendly interactions and increasing trust between human and bird. Food rewards can be used to reinforce good behavior.

THE DEVELOPMENT OF BEHAVIOR

The goal in socializing a baby parrot is to produce an adult that is neither fearful nor aggressive, noisy nor quiet, an adult that enjoys spending time alone, but is ready to "rock and roll" when others, including humans, seek interplay. There must be a balance of interaction and independence, cooperation and confidence.

Attention and Reinforcement

Birds need attention and reinforcement for effective transition to a new environment, to learn what they need to know to be parrots, and to develop a sense of security. The amount of attention and reinforcement needed for each bird is unique and particular to that bird. If the neonate was housed in a clear-sided brooder, if the youngster was rushed during the weaning process, or if it was not allowed to fledge, it may need more hours of direct interaction to develop healthy behavior. A baby parrot must learn several important skills such as eating, climbing, flapping, chewing, and playing independently in addition to cuddling.

The period between fledging and sexual maturity is the time of life during which a

Some parrots' territorial behavior is related to height.

parrot learns most quickly. Your parrot becomes an "information sponge." The onset of this period can be linked to physical development, as the arrival of physical coordination facilitates exploration. The bird has an almost compulsive desire to examine every detail of every aspect of life. The environment should be rich in colors and sounds and experiences. It should be like a nursery school. Limiting choices and experiences during this time limits the bird's intellectual and behavioral development and results in a poorly socialized parrot.

The young bird will be trying to copy the behavior of those around it and will be improvising the closest possible behavior. If nobody shows the bird what to do, it might follow the time-tested path so many companion parrots have tried before: taking over. This phenomenon is especially prominent and swift moving in Quaker parrots. It is often seen in companion cockatoos, Yellow-headed Amazons (especially yellow napes), Poicephalus, Caiques, and

The First Principle of Companion Parrot Behavior Management

Premium baby parrots don't usually come into the home biting, although they may have exploratory uses of the beak. As a young bird acclimates to the home, it becomes increasingly territorial, confident, experimental, and exploratory. This is noticeable to humans as juvenile beaks grow both stronger and harder. Most young parrots are quite delighted with the process and the results of using the beak, which can be troubling if the bird figures out that it is really fun to watch humans jump when beak is applied to flesh.

While consistent rewards may be required to establish a new behavior, intermittent rewards are a very strong way to reinforce randomly occurring behaviors. For this reason, once a bird has been rewarded even once for an unwanted random behavior, it can be difficult to make that behavior go away again. Often, after nips and bites have been accidentally reinforced, the parrots, themselves, tell us where the unintentional reinforcement came from. Accidentally rewarding experi-

mental beak use can result, later, in a bird that nips or bites hands, lips, or forearms, painfully, and then laughs. This behavior is commonly reported in Amazons, cockatoos, Quakers, conures, and Poicephalus. Many full-sized and mini macaws take great delight in performing this interaction.

The frequent appearance of this behavior, I believe, demonstrates well that the laughter of the favorite person is the preferred reward for companion parrots. Laughter is also easier to deliver than food rewards. Unfortunately, it is also easy to accidentally laugh, thereby accidentally rewarding amusing, but unwanted behavior.

If you don't want your parrot
to learn to bite,
**NEVER LAUGH WHEN YOUR BIRD
BITES YOUR SPOUSE**

It also helps if everybody learns to interact in ways that don't provoke the bird to bite.

lories, but can be seen in almost any type of parrot, even the tiniest ones.

Establishing Good Habits

Good socialization is a matter of reinforcing only those behaviors we wish to see again, and "reinforcement" to a happy young parrot can be almost anything.

1. The first form of reinforcement a bird encounters is *comfort.* Even before the egg hatches, parrot parents can hear their babies and are stimulated to sit on the egg, to provide

warmth and comfort for the developing embryo. If they don't hear a baby inside the egg, they might choose not to take care of the egg, and it won't hatch.

2. Upon hatching, the neonatal bird encounters *food* as a reward for vocalizing and actively competing to be fed. This new reward is reinforced by the familiar feelings of comfort. Food will remain a significant reinforcer throughout most parrots' lifetimes.

3. A parrot also develops *self-reward,* that is, doing what feels good because it feels good.

In an adult human, this would be like spending money, assembling a jigsaw puzzle, or playing golf.

4. Because they are highly social, *interaction* with other creatures also stimulates feelings of comfort in a parrot. Almost any kind of interaction, vocal or physical, can become a reward for behavior. This can be problematic, however, as many baby birds love interaction so much that any attention might be interpreted by the bird as a reward for the previous behavior.

Every effort should be made to stimulate and reinforce only positive behaviors in the young parrot. A companion parrot needs access to many different independent behavioral opportunities. Intermittent rewards for quietly playing alone help to establish independence as routine, habitual. It is also important not to reinforce negative behaviors, such as stealing eyeglasses off of strangers' faces or screaming when people leave the room, no matter how cute they seem the first time we see them.

Biting Prevention

Most early "beak on skin" activity is experimental behavior in which the young bird tries jaw muscles in combination with the beak for their effect. The bird must learn just how much pressure to exert on any given object to obtain the desired result. Much interest and devotion is given to this educational process. When the youngster exerts too much pressure on skin, care must be taken that the response is neither enjoyable nor provocative to the young bird. If the response to the bite is fun for the bird, the biting may become permanent. If the response excites the bird, it could provoke increased or continued aggression.

The best response to baby nibbles is to divert the beak to a different object such as a hand-held toy. If there is nothing to immediately replace in the bird's beak, then just put the bird down. A social young bird that knows attention will be easily withheld learns different behavior if different behavior is provided.

Cooperation Patterning

Any enjoyable interaction between human and bird can function to establish cooperation in the bird's set of behaviors. The most practical and easily accessible exercises for accomplishing this are peek-a-boos, step-ups, and the towel game.

Peek-a-boos

Peek-a-boos are easiest because you don't have to be near the bird or even in the same room. You can just peek around a corner and say something cute and appropriate such as, *"Peek-a-boo!"* or *"Peek-a-bird!"* This game is universal, played by juvenile animals of all kinds.

Step-up

To reinforce a more direct interaction, frequent stimulation and reinforcement of the bird's stepping-up response during the first weeks in the home lays the groundwork for future peaceful handling. The bird should enjoy stepping onto and off a hand as well as onto and off a hand-held perch. If the bird doesn't step up easily at or near the cage, then practice this activity in neutral (unfamiliar) territory.

Be sure to offer the perch where the legs join the belly so it can be most easily reached with the feet, rather than in front of the beak.

Be sure to maintain eye contact rather than looking at the hand approaching the bird. If the bird is maintaining eye contact and you look at your hand, the bird will look at your hand. If the bird looks at the approaching hand, it might either bite or flee rather than step-up.

A companion parrot should not have access to preventable behaviors such as chewing fragile furniture or accessories.

All cooperation patterning must be enjoyable to the bird. Daily practice of this interaction establishes the teacher as a flock member who should be looked to as a model for learning behavior. The step-up response must be so well entrenched that the bird will automatically perform the behavior, even if it is focused on biting, stealing a ring, sitting in a treetop, or being rescued from a fire. The bird should be so well practiced that when you say *"Step-up,"* no matter what is happening, it will immediately discontinue whatever it is doing and lift that foot!

Building Confidence with Choices

Especially during this time of rapid learning, the bird must be given access to appropriate choices. Selecting from various alternatives provides intellectual stimulation and confidence-building experience that enable the bird to overcome fear of new people, places, and things in the future.

A properly weaned young parrot comes with a taste for a variety of foods. Try not to reduce or limit the number of choices of foods offered, although quantities must be limited to prevent eating only favored foods. Now is the best time to encourage the bird to make other types of decisions, as well.

All cooperation patterning must be enjoyable for the bird.

The Towel Game

Baby companion parrots are hatched and nurtured in small, dark cavities. Snuggling in the furry folds of a towel should create feelings of safety and comfort for a young parrot. Many baby companion birds come with a natural enjoyment of being carried around nestled in a towel similar to the way one might carry a kitten or a doll. "Nestled" is the key word here; snuggling and nestling might involve confining the bird in the towel, but it doesn't mean wrapping it in the towel in a way in which its body is restrained, as for veterinary examinations.

The goal here is to replicate the feeling of security of being under Mommy's wings, but any baby can move around under Mommy's wing. The object is to get the bird to sit still voluntarily within the loose confines of the towel or quilt.

If the bird is initially afraid of the towel, try playing with the bird in the covers of the bed. This is a great time to practice gently touching the bird. Within a short time, many, but not all, birds will allow petting of any known-to-be-enjoyable place if only the head or eyes are covered. (Favorite places often include the neck, nostrils, top of the head, around the eyes, the oil gland, the wing pit, and the hollow under the mandible.)

Caution: Be sure not to fall asleep when playing snuggle games with the bird in the bed as the bird could easily suffocate if it crawls into the wrong position.

Patterning with this interaction should be encouraged, reinforced, and continued as long as the bird enjoys it, preferably for life.

Especially towel game patterning must be enjoyable for the bird.

This not only facilitates veterinary examinations and grooming, it can be an excellent calming and socialization tool as the bird grows older. Don't forget to have the humans wear the towels, hide their own heads and faces in the towels, and play peek-a-boo with each other and with the bird from behind the towels.

It is important, therefore, for a bird to have appropriate options about how and where it spends its time and numerous toys with which to play. Even if a bird chooses not to play on a small second perch joined to its main play area by a rope, or if it decides not to play with a particular toy, the presence of the second toy or play area has provided an opportunity for "successful" decision making.

Access to a choice of multiple activities supports the development of curiosity as well as confidence, encouraging the bird to explore the alternatives of an ever-changing world. The bird should have access *only* to appropriate choices for reasons of safety and so that unwanted behavior cannot be inadvertently reinforced. That is, the cage is not positioned beside a shelf of valuable miniatures or an expensive picture frame, but rather, the shelf should hold bird toys, and the wall, likewise, should hold a hanging piece of parrot-chewable "art" (a bird toy, of course).

In an inadequately designed environment, it is possible for a young parrot to find lots of unacceptable things to do, and Mom/Dad can wind up yelling *"Don't!"* or *"Stop it!"* all the time. Constant corrections can be damaging to a young parrot's behavior just as even well-intentioned criticism can damage children. Although it is counterintuitive, it is far better to suggest good behavior by saying *"Be a good bird!"* which can distract away from unwanted behavior and then offer an appropriate alternative activity such as chewing on a toy (see Detour Compliance, page 58).

Coming Out of the Cage

A companion parrot needs to feel that it has choices in the matter of interaction with humans, as well. Not everybody feels like interacting all the time. While it is important that a confident bird be patterned to step up from inside the cage, this is not always feasible with shyer birds. And, just because a bird will step up on the hand from inside the cage, that doesn't mean that anytime humans want the bird to come out, they simply require it.

I believe that a companion parrot should have the right to choose to come out of the cage, or not, by it's own choice. An especially shy or fearful bird should not be required to come out for nonemergency interactions if it chooses not to do so. Just open the cage door. A bird that wants to come outside, climbs to the top of the door or to the top of the cage and can be picked up there. If it does not come out, if it is eating or playing or for any other reason does not want to come out, you simply step away. Just be sure the bird does come out of the cage from time to time, even if that means sometimes feeding the bird on top of the cage.

The Shy Bird

Any behavior that is repeated can become a part of the bird's regular routine of behaviors. If naturally cautious parrots, especially, are repeatedly confronted in ways that stimulate and reinforce shyness, they will become increasingly fearful. Shy, cautious, or fearful birds must be permitted to hide whenever they choose. You must carefully discontinue eye contact and do everything you can to avoid stimulating the bird's instinct to fight or flee.

If you see a trend of developing fearfulness, you must take action to improve the bird's confidence, perhaps allowing it to live higher (or lower depending upon the bird), allowing

The Lifeguard Principle

It just feels right to say what *not to do*, what you don't want someone to do. But hasn't it been proved that just saying the words suggests the behavior? A No Smoking sign reminds some people that they'd like a smoke, a No Running sign reminds a happy child that it's fun to run.

Modern behavior managers now teach lifeguards to say, *"Slow down"* or *"Get in the pool."*

Most people find this more difficult to do than it sounds. It is counterintuitive. It feels more natural to say *"No, don't bite,"* but saying the word "bite" can stimulate, suggest, or reinforce the behavior. It has been well documented that naming a behavior does call it to mind, and does, for better or worse, stimulate the desire to engage in the behav-ior. This is especially true of parrots. A bird told that it is a "good bird" or a "pretty bird" is stimulated to engage in behaviors that it associates with those words.

The words, *"Be careful"* can also be established to distract from unwanted behavior in this way: Whenever you see that the bird is going to fall or is about to drop something or some other unwanted occurrence is about to take place, say *"Be careful."* The words *"Be careful"* become a termination stimulus. The bird will learn to stop, evaluate the situation, then continue with what it was doing or go on to another task. Eventually, if you see that a bird is about to bite, those words—*"Be careful"*—can terminate the unwanted behavior and help you redirect the bird's behavior.

---

it to choose whether to leave the cage on its own, or providing a place to hide. A little fabric tent, or just a towel over one end of the cage can provide a sense of security for a cautious companion parrot. While you might see an increase in territorial aggression around this ersatz nest site, this is exactly what you want to see when treating a shy bird. You will seldom treat fearfulness successfully without seeing at least a small increase in nippiness or a short biting phase. This is actually a sign that the bird is developing confidence.

The Parrot's Need to Play

A parrot in the wild is never at a loss for what to do. The tasks that are essential for the bird's continued existence allow for little spare time, and that is filled by playing with other birds. A captive parrot never has to learn all the things it was designed to do. An indoor parrot must learn indoor-acceptable activities that will help it cope with captive life and to avoid the behavior problems associated with the frustration of not knowing what to do with its time. Humans may have to teach the parrot how to play, and many humans have lost the knack or never learned to play.

Toys

Toys are tools for self-rewarding activities. We would like to do the same with the bird as we would do with a child, that is, hand the toy over and say, *"Here, play with this."*

Access to multiple successful choices creates and reinforces confidence and exploration in the bird's personality.

Unfortunately, birds will often ignore or be fearful of toys if they have not learned the benefits of chewing, banging, and shredding the objects hanging in the cage. Given a rich, stimulating, ever-changing environment, a young bird usually takes to this naturally, quickly, and with gusto.

If play behaviors don't develop in a young bird, they might not develop in that bird at all. A cautious young parrot might need special encouragement from its owner. Either of the following two suggestions are usually all that is necessary to generate play behaviors in a young, healthy parrot.

1. The human play gym. The bird's favorite person attaches toys to an old sweatshirt and wears it while holding the bird. Just as birds are often drawn to chew on buttons and jewelry, the bird will probably start chewing on the toys. Invite your friends, neighbors, and spouse to play with the toys. Delighted coos and praises from the favorite human will encourage the parrot to play with the toys. The same toys can be put into the cage before the bird is returned to it. Again, praise the bird when it explores a toy in order to encourage it to continue playing independently.

2. "Keep away." This is an excellent game for piquing a parrot's interest in a new toy or new food. This game is played by showing the bird the toy or food only very briefly; the bird is not allowed to see the toy long enough to become afraid of it. Then the favorite human

Toys are tools for self-rewarding behavior.

A wild parrot is never bored.

can show excitement over having the toy and begin playing with it.

If the toy can be shredded, the person should shred it a bit. If it can be eaten, the person should eat some, all while the bird can watch. Show the object to the bird again. Give it to a rival that will enjoy it. Show it to the bird again. Play with it again. Eventually the bird will start leaning closer and closer to try to find out what it is. By the time the bird is given the object, it will be very excited to have it. Most birds will succumb to curiosity within a few minutes. Some birds may take several sessions.

Bright Objects

Some birds may prefer objects that are not bright and colorful. Shredded paper, twigs, natural rope, or vegetable-tanned leather may be more interesting to some birds than fancy expensive toys. Pompoms made from newspaper or some other paper that is not shiny can be irresistible to some birds. Weaving paper, leather, or bias-cut cloth in and out of the cage bars near the bird's favorite perch can draw a bird into chewing. Bundles of twigs might be attached to the sides of the cage. Branches where the bark is already starting to peel can replace plain perches.

Fear of New Toys

Birds that are simply afraid of new toys can get used to them while they are lying near the cage. The toys can be gradually moved closer and even hung on the outside of the cage. Toys hung on the outside of the cage that have parts that can be pulled inside can be especially enticing and challenging.

"Keep away" also helps these birds overcome their fears. Once a bird has seen many new toys, it will usually start to welcome new additions. Then comes the challenge of finding a toy that survives more than a few minutes before being destroyed.

Side-by-Side and Face-to-Face Activities

It is easy for a young feathered darling to come to expect constant emotional reinforcement or face-to-face interaction. When we're talking directly to the bird, one on one, when we're holding or petting the bird, we can do nothing else. Our attention is held captive. This behavior is easily adopted by juvenile cockatoos and African Greys, but any human-bonded hand-fed baby parrot can become strongly entrenched in this behavior.

While the young bird needs face-to-face interaction, quality social time with a companion parrot also means sharing side-by-side activities such as eating, bathing, talking, singing, exercising, and expressing affection with other humans in the presence of the bird. The bird learns autonomous behavior by seeing it and copying it. This leads to the development of independence. Extreme *independence*, where little or no interactions with humans are necessary sometimes occurs in budgies, ringnecks, grass parakeets, Poicephalus, loris, and cockatiels. Extreme *dependence* can develop easily in cockatoos, African Greys, eclectus, macaws, and almost any hand-fed parrot that is reinforced in dependence to the exclusion of independence, exploration, and curiosity.

Side-by-side, indirect social activities can also be helpful in bonding with a shy or cautious bird. Even if it doesn't enjoy being handled, a parrot still has a compelling need to spend time with a social group. I have seen many difficult-to-correct behavioral problems develop in birds that are not allowed to see the human "flock" eat and birds that cannot, because of their location, see what humans are watching (usually the television).

Bonding and Territorialism

Following cycles of exploratory behavior, you will see the beginnings of the development of a protective attitude toward territory—both actual territory and human "territory." This protective or territorial behavior might be related to a place, such as the dining room or kitchen counter, or it might be related to a situation, such as height. It might be related to nearness to humans, such as the back of the sofa, or it might be part of the favorite person, such as the shoulder or lap.

Many companion parrots decide that a reflective surface is either a mate or a rival, leading to many courtships with toasters and wars with hair dryers. A sexually mature companion parrot might decide that no one is allowed in the kitchen. It is important to keep in mind that a bird that has fixated on a human-owned object or territory must be denied access to them. An attacking bird might be picked up using a hand-held perch, a towel, or "Distraction Devices" (see page 51) and placed with the toy it likes most to beat up, which becomes an approved surrogate "enemy." Parrots have a tremendous amount of energy. Indoors, that energy often comes out when expressing territorialism. This warlike, defensive, or hostile energy must be expressed somehow; it is best expressed against a toy.

It is important at this time to move the bird's cage occasionally, to rearrange and change toys periodically, and to guide the bird to maintain interactions with more than one person.

Overcoming Territorialism

Cooperation patterning, such as step-ups are a helpful tool in overcoming territorialism as you train the bird to be ferried or transported from one place to another in the well-planned environment. The bird should have at least two regular areas in which to spend time: a roost cage in which to sleep (see page 30), and one or more "foraging" area(s). The bird should be dependent upon humans to get from one area to another by stepping onto the hand to get

What Is a Bite Anyway?

A parrot's beak functions as its hand for holding onto things, as well as its sense of touch. So when a parrot reaches with its beak, it does not automatically mean the bird plans to hurt you. Following is Liz' Wilson's description of common uses of a companion parrot's beak.

Action	Physical Reaction on Human Anatomy
Touching/"Tasting"	No damage or possibly a tiny bit of redness on the skin, a plucked hair, or removed scab
Nipping/ Pinching	Redness, possibly a mark from the beak
Bite	Bruise or small cut, possibly a small amount of bleeding
Chomp	Deep bruise or cut with lots of bleeding

from the cage to the perch or shower every day. This "transportation dependence" helps the bird to understand that successful interactions with humans are rewarded with interesting, exciting things to do.

Preferences for One Person or Gender

Territorialism related to a person or gender can be especially troubling. Although the bird will often, but not always, demonstrate an obvious preference for one person over another, a young bird that expresses aggression against a less-favored person might change loyalties as more adult behavior develops and begin attacking the previously favored person. Bond switches and periodically changing loyalties are reported in African Greys, cockatoos, Amazons, and conures, but I believe there is potential for this behavior in any parrot that is allowed to bite or chomp on all but the favorite person. Occasional outings where the bird is handled by sensitive, astute, less-than-favorite humans can be used to manipulate bonding behaviors, improve patterning, and reduce territorialism.

Sexual Displays

Be sure not to reinforce sexual displays, such as strutting and fanning Amazons, that may become increasingly territorial during display. Be sure not to pet the bird in a manner that stimulates a sexual response, especially cockatoos, which often respond to under-the-wing body petting in a sexual manner.

The bird should interact with numerous "regulars" and "strangers." A companion parrot should attend as many human gatherings as possible in a safe and structured way. If the young bird expresses "dislike" of one person, and it can be determined that the bird's responses are not related to the signals or body language of that person, then efforts can be made to improve the relationship with that person. This is not usually true "dislike" of a person, but rather an expression of territorial instinct that stimulates the bird to try to drive away all but its favorites.

Phases Come and Go

In human infants, it is well known that periods of fussiness often accompany transitions or

A companion parrot might develop territorialism related to a person or a gender.

parrot might get a little noisy immediately before she finally figures out how to say *"Commere"* or fly across the room.

A juvenile parrot is often irritable when it is growing in new feathers, especially wing feathers, for the first time. Whether the "irritable" period is marked by screaming, begging vocally for attention, or nipping, the best way to deal with it is to stimulate a different behavior that can then be reinforced. Cathy Isbell calls this "Detour Compliance" (see page 58).

precede great leaps in learning, such as when a baby can crawl over and reach a toy rather than scream for someone to hand it over. Likewise, juvenile parrots that are on the verge of making great learning strides can go through periods of cranky behavior immediately before taking those crucial steps. Jacquie the Jardine's

Allowing Aggression

Territorial aggression can develop if the bird is allowed to establish dominance on the human shoulder. Any parrot that will not immediately and peacefully comply with a step-up prompt when on the shoulder can severely damage human eyes, ears, and lips. The baby parrot needs to know that you are a loving benefactor, not "territory" to be defended.

An unweaned or under-six-month-old parrot that is already threatening and biting people and/or inanimate objects, must be given sound behavioral backup immediately, as this can be a sign of serious problems developing. Aggression in an unweaned or newly weaned bird can be unintentionally reinforced as the bird's personality is being formed. If it is repeatedly reinforced, that aggression will escalate. Don't hesitate if you think you might need profes-

A parrot might develop territorial behavior related to the shoulder.

sional assistance. A parrot behavior consultant is little different from a horse trainer, and most people who have had a horse have probably used the services of a trainer at one time or another.

Fearfulness

Fearfulness may also be a passing phase with many young parrots. Just be careful not to be stimulating fear reactions on an ongoing basis. Transitional fearfulness may appear as a specific response to one person. If that is the case, try to figure out what stimulated the first enactment of the response and be careful not to repeat that interaction.

Companion parrots should attend as many human gatherings as possible in a safe and structured way.

Pinning, the opening and closing of the iris that denotes excitement, can be seen easily on birds with yellow eyes.

Chewing Behaviors

By two to three years of age, most parrots will be exhibiting chewing behaviors. You will see a transition from a time when toys were hardly scratched, through a time when they are dismantled into parts, to a time when they are completely demolished into splinters. As these behaviors develop, it is necessary to increase the number and frequency of chewables in the restricted environments of both the cage and the play area.

New Behaviors

As with human children, new behaviors will seem to appear from nowhere. For months, the bird will leave the picture frame behind the cage alone. Then one day, the picture frame is splintered on two sides. For years, the bird might put nothing into the water, then one day it will begin filling the water bowl with debris. A maturing parrot might suddenly begin pulling newspaper up through the grate. These behaviors are probably part of the parrot's instinctive drive to reproduce; the bird is doing what it was "programmed" to do. You must provide other appropriate things to chew and reinforce the bird for chewing appropriately.

As the Bird Matures

As in other creatures, the instinct to reproduce is the parrot's strongest instinct. Unlike companion dogs and cats that are spayed and/or neutered for behavioral reasons, companion parrots are allowed the full influence of their reproductive urges. A parrot expressing this very real natural instinct might chew the stereo speakers to splinters, decide to allow no one near the breakfast nook, regurgitate on your house slippers, or masturbate on the dog.

Instead of surgically altering the animal, you must learn to stimulate different behavior. The techniques described in this book are intended to enhance favorable behaviors for human/avian interaction and to suppress or minimize most behaviors related to breeding.

It is tremendously important to continue interacting with the maturing companion parrot regularly in order to maintain tameness. Some birds will be easily kept tame; some will be difficult. Expect every bird to be a little different, with vast differences between species and between successfully socialized birds and unsocialized birds of the same species. The more consistent you are in all interactions, the more predictable the bird will be.

As the time to breed approaches, you will see heightened exploration and physical and emotional experimentation. The bird might even change emotional and/or territorial loyalties, becoming aggressive around a newly selected territory or a new favorite human (mate substitute). If a parrot has been allowed to overbond to one human in the past, at this time, the formerly favorite human might be dumped for a more easily dominated companion. You *must* be ever vigilant to ensure that the bird is not excessively defensive of the territory around any human so that previous and predictable loyalties will not be abandoned.

Of course, just because a companion parrot is exhibiting sexual behaviors does not mean that it would be "better off breeding." It is no more appropriate to suddenly stick a human-bonded companion parrot into an all-parrot breeding world than it is to require a teenager to marry because you caught him masturbating.

Distraction Devices

A bird might begin to bite even a well-placed hand prompt for the step-up command. The most common time for a nip or bite of a hand offered for step-ups is when the bird is being removed from a familiar perch, human, top of the cage, or when it is being returned to the cage. This behavior can usually be defeated with distraction, practice, a hand-held perch, improved technique, or more frequent step-up practice in unfamiliar territory.

✔ Sometimes a distraction device is necessary to keep the bird from looking at the hand approaching for the step-up. Maintain eye contact and offer the hand to be stepped on, approaching from below, as usual. Just as the prompt hand begins its approach to the bird, present an unfamiliar object just out of reach of the bird's beak (with one hand) and give the *"step up"* command (with the other hand) followed by *"Be a good bird."*

✔ If a bird is threatening to bite the hand you want it to step on, you can pick up a small object (a spoon or a telephone or piece of junk mail) and hold it about an inch below and in front of the bird's beak, give the step-up command, and suggest good behavior. Usually the surprised bird, responding to the familiar behavioral pattern, and knowing what "Good bird" means, responds also by being what it is expected to be—a good bird.

✔ Eye contact is especially important here. A bird will often maintain eye contact rather than bite. If the bird's eye is distracted by the introduced object, it will seek to regain eye contact immediately rather than take the time to bite after being distracted.

✔ Even if the bird bites, that unfamiliar object, rather than the hand being offered, will probably be bitten. A clean new wooden spoon or hand-held toy works well for this. Care must be taken to ensure that the distraction device is not frightening to a shy parrot. The distraction object must be neither too large, which might frighten the bird, too small, which might be ineffective, nor toxic (a lead or painted object) if the bird chooses to receive the object and chew on it.

It might be necessary to take a feisty young bird out of its familiar territory for at least a few days each year in order to repattern the bird and to facilitate interactions with unfamiliar humans. Vacations and indoor "outings," such as visits to unfamiliar territory, are very helpful at this time. Even a simple car ride with the bird in a carrier can make a wonderful difference in a parrot's disposition. Careful transporting and meticulous wing feather trims ensure safety on these outings.

Control Issues

At home the maturing parrot will become increasingly concerned with control issues, especially immediate environmental control. The bird might decide to defend a height territory, sofa, or floor territory. It might start attacking toes or tissues, or people sneezing or blowing their noses into tissues. A maturing parrot might also attack anyone cleaning with quick motions with paper towels. You should remove the bird from the area before

Parrots allowed on the floor can become territorial and begin attacking feet.

Parrots should always have a secure place to perch.

A cockatiel that is handled frequently from an early age is unlikely to develop aggressive behavior.

Parrots kept in multiples may develop breeding-related behaviors—such as screaming—that humans may consider invasive.

Two parrots enjoy resting on a tree branch.

cleaning so that these behaviors are not reinforced.

Liberty in the Home

A maturing parrot allowed a great deal of liberty in the home might become hypervigilant or aggressive around a suddenly and mysteriously selected territory. Expect heightened reactions to mirrors, shiny objects, and small appliances. It might attack the vacuum cleaner or hair dryer. It will be seeking both companions and interlopers in its reflections. At this time the bird might fixate strongly on an inanimate object, treating it either as a potential mate or as an enemy to be attacked.

Selecting a Surrogate "Enemy"

There must be at least one enemy who can be regularly thwarted. To a very real extent, the bird must "select" or "identify" this enemy independently. Most parrots will do this. Of course, it is very important for this enemy not to be a living creature or a treasured human possession, so several potential approved "surrogate enemies" must be provided. Unbreakable hanging toys or loud, safe bells are excellent candidates for this parrot-selected "enemy." If a companion parrot has no opportunity to release natural aggressive energy against an approved surrogate enemy at this time, the bird is likely to begin to express that "excess" energy against whatever or whoever is closest.

If the bird is enjoying attacking a toy, leave them both alone. There will be many times when the bird will solicit human attention. Those are the times when even a mature bird can be successfully patterned to cooperate with the redundant use of praise and rewards. The more successful behavioral experiences we have, and the more the bird is patterned and reinforced to cooperate, the more likely the bird will remain cooperative.

Dealing with Aggression

There will come a time when threats might be accompanied by aggression; a bite might actually break the skin. A sexually mature parrot, especially a teenage cockatoo, is usually more difficult to handle than a strutting little adolescent whose challenges are mere practice. At this time, new programs, people, and changes might be met with resistance. If, however, the bird has been acclimated to accept change, the bird's behavior might be maintained merely by manipulating the environment.

If a parrot has not been patterned to cooperate and acclimated to change by the teen years, attempts to socialize or resocialize may be overridden by the bird's instincts to reproduce and by the habitual self-rewarding behaviors that have developed. During the teen years a parrot might develop both predictable and unpredictable biting behavior, especially in the perceived territory. Usually there will be plenty of warning: hypervigilance, eye movement, wing or tail display, charging with beak open, or any other body language that usually accompanies aggression in a particular individual.

The best way to deal with aggression in a sexually mature companion parrot is to avoid the issue. Do whatever is necessary to stimulate the bird to different behavior. Never allow the bird to chase or harass. Merely remind the bird to *"be a good bird,"* then return it to the cage in the calmest possible way. A bird being prompted to step up might be distracted with a toy or other inanimate object when being given the prompt for step-up.

You might also choose to handle an otherwise well-adapted bird either with the towel or with hand-held perches during nippy stages. Don't discontinue interactions; only discontinue any interactions that might involve nipping or biting. Try the games starting on page 9 of Barron's *Guide to a Well-behaved Parrot* by Mattie Sue Athan. Hone your own skills at Detour Compliance (see page 58). Careful techniques by everyone who interacts with the bird are necessary to maintain tameness here, for if the bird has no chance to bite, biting can't be reinforced.

Sexual Behavior

Even solitary companion parrots can develop sexual behaviors. Although many companion parrots will limit "sexual" behaviors to courtship behaviors, including chewing, eating, and feeding, many birds will more overtly seek to gratify their natural instincts. Expect to see masturbation in many, perhaps most, healthy male birds and in a high percentage of female birds. A companion parrot might solicit copulation from a favorite human or engage in masturbation, a masturbation display, or anxiety behaviors that sometimes include sexual gestures.

Each bird's masturbation process is accompanied by that species' characteristic sexual sounds. An astute owner can tell what's going on by hearing that particular sound that is made only at that time. My own hen cockatiel Pearl, who neither talks nor whistles at other times, whistles a typical male cockatiel song as she masturbates, tail up in the corner of her cage.

It is probably not a good idea to encourage masturbation behaviors as they can be accompanied by aggression or feather picking. In addition, a companion bird that habitually engages in masturbation behaviors may later choose those behaviors over mating even if a mate is offered. Just ignore these behaviors; don't reinforce them. If the behaviors don't get attention and aren't reinforced, they're less likely to reappear. However, since self-gratification is the very definition of self-rewarding behavior, masturbation behaviors may continue regardless of whether they are reinforced by humans or not.

Exaggerated chewing, allofeeding, or regurgitation are also commonly seen sexual behaviors. If the bird is regurgitating on humans, just put it down—this is neither to be rewarded nor discouraged.

BEHAVIOR MANAGEMENT

If a companion parrot learns one new annoying, intrusive, or unhealthy behavior yearly, it will be pretty difficult to live with by the end of its first decade. Successful companion parrot homes resolve each behavioral issue as it appears, lest an accumulation of unwanted behaviors push the bird into isolation in a garage or back room or into another home.

A normal, healthy companion parrot goes through many exploratory phases. Some of the behaviors it explores will be accidentally rewarded by humans, and the bird will become increasingly adept at rewarding its own behavior. A companion parrot can develop behaviors that are very enjoyable for the bird but may be troubling to humans. Typical issues involving unwanted behavior include annoying vocalizations, inappropriate use of the beak on skin, and feather-damaging behaviors.

Strategies and Timing

The secret to managing unwanted behavior is planning strategies to elicit wanted behavior so that it can then be reinforced. Were it not for the strength and force of habits, this would

Early planning and good practice will prevent the development of unwanted behaviors as a parrot matures.

be easy but habits are tenacious things that can be very difficult to change. When you are working to change a habit, you must find ways to stimulate behavior that is so much fun that the bird chooses to do that instead of the comfortable old behavior. This can be challenging. Once any creature learns to do something, it is very difficult to *unlearn* it, especially if that something is occasionally rewarded in any way. It becomes even more important *never* to accidentally reinforce unwanted behavior, even occasionally, as intermittent rewards are the strongest rewards for continuing already occurring behavior.

Timing is especially important when dealing with unwanted established behaviors, because the new behavior has to be stimulated just before the unwanted behavior would typically be enacted. For example, if you want to change unwanted screaming, you have to keep a diary in order to figure out when the bird will scream, then provide something else for it to do during the time it would be screaming. The replacement behavior must be so compelling, so interesting, that a bird will choose to do it instead of a habitual behavior. This is possible only *if* humans are willing and able to make changes in their own behavior. There must be teamwork; every member of the household must be consistent in reinforcing wanted behaviors and ignoring unwanted ones.

Detour Compliance: Stimulating and Reinforcing Alternative Interactions

We've all heard that "the shortest distance between two points is a straight line."

It is what our intuition tells us. We want to take the shortest, fastest course and we become agitated if anything interferes. Cathy Isbell tells a story about a road near her home that is closed by floods every year. There are roadblocks and detour signs everywhere, but at least one driver yearly refuses to detour, choosing instead to cross that flooded road. The car, sometimes the driver, is swept away by a river that was once the road.

Many people take this same attitude with parrots, forging ahead when the signs say "Detour," forcing interaction in confrontational ways that destroy trust. While face-to-face conflict with a parrot might not be as dangerous as driving a car into a river, it can have disastrous results. It can establish a pattern of mistrust that becomes a permanent fixture in the bird's behavior.

The most direct way to get a parrot to do something may not be the best way. If you notice that a request is met with fear or aggression, stop and rethink your approach. Change course. I call this stimulating an *alternative behavior*. Cathy Isbell calls it "Detour Compliance."

There is a big difference between a truly aggressive or fearful response and a hesitant one. A bird might simply be testing you. Parrots want to follow a successful leader. Sometimes all that is needed is a firm, self-assured restatement of the request for the bird to recognize you as a leader and comply with your request. Reasserting a request is not "Detour Compliance."

When the bird makes it known with posture, lunging, flailing, screaming, or even by saying, *"No,"* that it will not cooperate, it is time for a "detour." Think things through before taking action. Is this request necessary? If you want to play and the bird is not in the mood, there is no need to force the issue. However, if the bird needs to be taken to the veterinarian, you must get there in the most efficient and least stressful way possible.

For example, Salt and Pepper, the African Grey parrots, are deathly afraid of the plastic carrier they were transported in before they came to live with Cathy. They would flail and panic whenever they saw it. Putting them into this carrier would simply be too traumatic so she decided to try a little detour.

Cathy found a small travel cage with easily gripped perches and left it near their cage for several days. When it was time to go to the veterinarian, they went into the new cage without a fuss. They actually enjoyed the trip, talking and singing all the way. They were not forced to accept the old carrier but rather were offered an alternative. They enjoyed a happy

CHECKLIST

Why Parrots Bite and What to Do About It

1 Fear or anxiety biting is generated by the instinct to fight or fly away especially when complicated by containment, trimmed wings, or the perception of no choice in the matter.
✔ Don't force the bird to do anything unnecessary.
✔ Address fear biting by being less confrontational and improving access to feelings of safety.
✔ Improve cooperation patterning using towel games, eye games, step-ups, or other nonthreatening strategies.
✔ Model cooperative behavior.
✔ Learn to stimulate and reinforce alternative behaviors.

2 Territorial biting to defend a mate, nest site, height, status, toys, food, or water includes displaced aggression, which is biting something or someone the bird can reach when it cannot reach the individual it wants to bite.
✔ Watch for signs of territorial biting, maintain eye contact, and put the bird down or use hand-held perches.
✔ Improve cooperation patterning and bonding with increased handling and outings. Look for ways to stimulate and reinforce different behavior.
✔ Don't let a parrot sit on your shoulder.

3 Manipulation biting is learned behavior the parrot uses to get its way, such as biting when the owner looks away, or is on the phone, or when being returned to the cage. This includes "test" biting taught by unsteady humans who offer a hand, then pull away and "drama-reward" biting where birds bite because they enjoy seeing humans scream and jump.
✔ Make the behavior obsolete by denying opportunities for the bird to do it. Behaviors that are not done cannot be reinforced into habits.
✔ Anticipate biting situations and avoid them. Improve cooperation patterning, techniques, or methods.
✔ Don't quit eye contact when answering the phone or returning the bird to the cage. Put the bird down before answering the phone.

4 The "wound-up" bird. Healthy parrots, especially Amazons and cockatoos can be overstimulated in a manner similar to hyperactive children at a family picnic.
✔ Train to a termination stimulus.
✔ Be sure the bird is getting enough sleep. It might be time for a nap when Peaches is slashing for the apparent joy of slashing.
✔ Consider adding a roost cage.
✔ Don't try to handle a bird that is overstimulated or aggressively playing with a toy.
✔ Use environment to distract from the behavior.
✔ Provide more opportunities for exercise and bathing.

experience and cemented an ever-more-trusting bond.

There are always alternatives. "Detour Compliance" might involve using a hand-held perch when a bird would otherwise nip a hand. It might mean passing a bird to a less-favored person by placing it first on a neutral or lower perch.

Make detours habitual. Anytime it looks like cooperation is not an option, step back, think again, and try something else. Take your time. If the bird is afraid of a hand-held perch, offer a long wooden ladder. If it is afraid of the ladder, try a basket handle. Ultimately, the time taken to circumvent fearful or aggressive responses saves heartache and loss of trust that might be difficult or impossible to regain.

Last, but far from least, "Detour Compliance" helps the handler learn confidence. You know you won't be hurt. You know you can handle any situation. You win. The bird wins. Every-

Parrot behavior can be changed if humans who influence that behavior can change.

body wins. Each successful detour repeats a pattern of cooperation and fewer and fewer detours are necessary.

The Termination Stimulus

When the alarm clock goes off in the morning, the sound it makes is not punishment; it is a termination stimulus, a signal that if you don't stop what you are doing (sleeping) and do something else (get up and go to work), something you don't want to happen will happen (you will lose your job). Likewise, an oven timer tells us that if we don't take the cake out of the oven, it will be burned; and a doorbell tells us that if we don't stop what we are doing and go to the door, the opportunity there will go away.

A termination stimulus can be a valuable tool in dealing with a bird that is engaging in unwanted behavior. Whether the bird is in the middle of an afternoon screaming jag, chewing on the blinds, or sliding down the corner of the cage eyeballing toes, a well-timed snap of the fingers or clap of the hands can signal that the behavior must be terminated or an unwanted consequence will occur—the bird might be returned to the cage or perch, or it might be given a short nap to "shift gears" to lower energy and less painful-to-humans behavior.

The "Evil Eye"

The most common termination stimulus is probably a stern and disapproving look—what Sally Blanchard calls the "evil eye." It is a way of reminding the bird to discontinue an unwanted behavior or the threat of apparently

A parrot can often be enticed to play with a favorite toy rather than scream when humans leave the room.

intended behavior. This process seems to work well in some birds, works not at all in other birds, and is too frightening for some birds. For some, a raised eyebrow is enough.

The "evil eye" might stimulate a fear response in sensitive parrots because it is similar to the straight-on, even-eyed gaze of a hunter. Parrots are prey species, animals that are killed for food, not predators. In prey species, the eyes are situated on the sides of the head, rather than on the front where human eyes are situated. This enables prey species to see danger approaching from beside or behind so that they can escape becoming someone's meal. When a bird is examining something with great interest, it looks first with one eye and then with the other eye. When approaching a shy or unfamiliar bird, use less threatening eye contact with one eye closer, nose pointed to the side of the bird.

Straight-on eye contact in the manner of a predator can "freeze" a knowing bird into

Alex's Game

African Grey parrots are known to frequently possess and display a great love of vocal tricks or games. The smarter the bird, the more potential there is for the bird to find ways to enjoy "tricking" humans. It would stand to reason, therefore, that Dr. Pepperberg's bird Alex probably knows a surprising number of tricks to play on humans. However, it hadn't occurred to me that a bird that lives in a university laboratory and that interacts daily with very intelligent, well-educated people would spend two days trying to trick me into breaking the rules.

I was very delighted to be invited to visit Alex, and after awkwardly negotiating the security and disinfectant procedures, Alex could immediately recognize me as a stranger, newcomer, outsider, and easy pickin's for mischief. There he was, standing flatfooted on his table; I was face-to-face with the World's Most Famous Grey parrot.

Regarding me through first one oblong, slitty eye, then another, Alex bobbed his head and treated me to a loud tonally correct wolf whistle. Both parts.

Then he stopped, looked again, and waited. I was just about puckered up to respond when Dr. Pepperberg put her hand on my arm and shook her head "No."

Alex immediately repeated only the first half of the wolf whistle, regarding me with expectant mischief in his eyes. Again, Dr. Pepperberg shook her head "No."

You see, those who study Alex's language skills know not to engage in whistling with Alex in the laboratory because it might interfere with his desire to use human words, which are more difficult to form. Newcomers are sometimes unaware of the rules, and Alex knows that they can sometimes be tricked into playing whistling games.

Again and again during the few treasured hours I visited, Alex tried to "sucker" me into a forbidden whistling game. It wasn't easy to ignore his charming, invitational whistles. It was very, very difficult to take Dr. Pepperberg's instruction, for Alex can be quite demanding in his quest for self-rewarding interactions. I guess he knows that all work and no play might make Alex a "dull boy." In fact, Dr. Pepperberg says that Alex is very dedicated in his quest for self-rewarding behaviors, spending many, many, more hours playing than "working."

stillness. Once the bird's actions have been stopped by the gaze, humans can then suggest an appropriate behavior to replace the unwanted activity. Be careful when using new or unpatterned devices such as this, as a straight-on gaze might be too frightening for some birds such as some African Greys, Poicephalus, cockatoos, and eclectus. Know your bird and its level of fearfulness before using the "evil eye."

Snapping Fingers or Clapping Hands

While the "evil eye" is a sort of naturally set-up termination stimulus, other signals can be used if they are properly reinforced. If the bird is eyeballing Aunt Verna's toes and you know toes have been bloodied before, snap your fingers or clap your hands to get the bird's attention. If the bird looks up and then directly back at those toes, just pick it up and return it to the cage or a perch or quickly provide a barrier between beak and toes. If the bird is very intent on what it is doing, you might have to pick it up with a hand-held perch or use a distraction device (see page 51) or some other detour from the intended behavior.

Objects as Termination Stimuli

The termination stimulus might also be an object, such as a towel to signal a rowdy bird on an afternoon screaming jag to terminate the behavior, lest it be treated to a nap (see Roost Cage, page 30).

Using Alternative Behavior

A termination stimulus is most effective when it is accompanied by direction to appropriate behavior, such as with the lifeguard principle (see page 43). Snap your fingers or clap your hands and say *"Be a good bird!"* The distraction of the clap can also be supplemented with the provision of an alternative behavior, such as handing the bird a toy. The bird soon learns to change behavior to avoid being returned to the cage.

The Influence of Environment

Since companion parrot behavior develops as a response to the indoor environment with its humans, its controlled temperature, artificial light, windlessness, treelessness, and lack of rain, the easiest way to change behavior is to change the environment. For example, raising

Help, My Rosie Is Sneezing!

Bert, a meticulous housekeeper, was allergic to dust. A tiny bit of the stuff sent him into a sneezing fit that might go on for several minutes. He'd done his homework, and he knew not to get a cockatoo or an African Grey because of the dust they produce. He wound up with Rosie, a red lori that dazzled friends with her color and acrobatics. Some of his friends even said that he wouldn't leave the house much after Rosie's arrival because he so much enjoyed watching his bird.

He had been warned that lories were especially sensitive, so he researched her needs and provided the right diet. He even bought a Vita-Mix, a top of the line blender, to prepare nutritious fruit mixes that he shared with the bird. His own diet improved. He lost weight, looked good, and felt great.

Three weeks after she moved into Bert's home and a week after a perfect well-baby exam, Bert noticed that Rosie was sneezing a few times every day. He'd never lived with a parrot before, and he was very concerned about her well-being. It seemed that every day, she was sneezing just a little more.

On a spring morning, Bert put Rosie into her carrier and drove across town to the veterinarian. As he walked into the doctor's office, Bert had one of his sneezing attacks. Rosie sneezed right along with him: sneeze for sneeze.

The laughing veterinarian and her staff looked at the happy posturing, pinning bird and her ten-day-old blood work and sent them home. Bert was relieved to learn that Rosie's sneezing was an indication of her bond with her human "flockmate," not an indication of ill health.

Flapping is a necessary and enjoyable activity for healthy companion parrots.

The laughter of the favorite person is the strongest reinforcer of companion parrot behavior.

or lowering the bird's usual relative height, combined with increasing access to bathing or shower opportunities, destructible chewables, and exercise can help to compensate for pent-up energy that might otherwise be expressed as aggression. Territorial behavior might be tempered by moving the cage or redesigning the cage interior by providing new perches and rotating toys periodically.

But humans are the most significant part of the companion parrot's environment, and humans can be very resistant to change. It is our responsibility to make the changes necessary to stimulate and reinforce harmony.

Vocalizations: The Ones We Want to Hear and the Ones We Don't

Body Sounds

Vocalizations are the most obviously human-influenced element of companion parrot behavior, as these incredible creatures learn to emulate and communicate with their human families. A parrot's ability to copy a sound influences the sounds it learns to make, but with that limitation, a companion parrot learns to repeat sounds that are made often and with enthusiasm. Indeed, many companion parrots pick up spontaneous and enthusiastic human body sounds—coughs, sneezes, belches, and laughter—before they learn human words.

Laughter: A new parrot companion is most likely to mimic sounds it associates with human happiness. Laughter is, apparently, especially easy for a parrot to learn, with many happy humans reporting that their bird is the only one

A parakeet might learn many human words, but might say them so quickly that they are difficult to understand.

that "catches onto" (laughs at) all their jokes. They are also attracted to redundant syllables and seem to favor words that end in "itty" sounds such as "pretty" and "kitty."

Whistling: The parrot's vocal mechanism resembles whistling, however, and much experimenting is usually required to make most natural vocalizations sound like words. A few are almost natural; "what" and "hi" seem to develop with little or no practice. Sometimes, whistling may be used as a "bridge" to learning words, but some birds so love to whistle that they might whistle rather than talk. This can become an especially interesting game such as the one played by Alex in Dr. Pepperberg's lab, as reported in Barron's *African Grey Parrot Handbook* by Mattie Sue Athan and Dianalee Deter.

Parrots often invent games to play with their humans.

Learning Words

While most parrots develop at least a few words, many parrots learn many more. The *Guinness Book of World Records* lists a budgie, the most common parrot, as having the greatest number of human words. But studies suggest that budgies use human words like calls and

CHECKLIST

The Most Common Types of Feather-Damaging Behaviors

✔ *Feather chewing* or *shredding* begins with injury to the edge of the feathers. This might be related to soiled feathers, boredom, falling, anxiety, feelings of abandonment, poor diet, or inadequate lighting. It is the most common form of self-inflicted damage,

✔ *Feather snapping* involves breaking the feather shaft. The shaft might be snapped near the outer end leaving feathers with a "V" shape, or it might be snapped near the base leaving no feathers visible outside the down. Down, too, might be snapped off.

✔ *Feather plucking* involves pulling feathers out, sometimes making the bird version of an *"ouch."* This might be ongoing or a temporary response to dirty or damaged feathers. Feather pulling is especially common around the vent or the preening gland at the base of the tail.

✔ *Feather picking* is a generic term commonly used to refer to self-inflicted feather chewing, shredding, snapping, or plucking.

are less likely to use words with association than African Greys, the only species that have been studied extensively in a laboratory setting. Many Amazons, macaws, Quakers, and ringnecks are good talkers. Many individuals of other species also learn to say human words and may learn to use them with appropriate association.

Songs or Calls

In addition to learned vocalizations, parrots come with natural vocalizations innate to the particular species. While many of these sounds in many birds might be described by humans as "song," most of the innate sounds parrots make should probably be described as "calls." Many humans would describe many parrot sounds as "screams." And therein lies the most commonly reported issue related to companion parrot vocalizations.

Only a small part of parrot vocalizations consists of quiet one-on-one vocalizations. Much of a parrot's wild language is intended to give information to the flock or family. Wake-up calls, come-to-dinner calls, where-are-you calls, and everybody-get-to-sleep calls must be loud enough for all to hear. Contact calls, used to keep in touch with a nearby out-of-sight mate or companion, are just loud enough to be heard and acknowledged.

Birds like saying things that are easy to say and easy to relate to. They can and do, apparently, enjoy using words in ways consistent with their meaning. Replacing a redundant unwanted call might be as simple as convincing the bird that some other call is more fun and more useful. For example, I was asked to help with Feather, an African Grey parrot that had acquired a hen cockatiel alarm call as a result of bird-sitting over the weekend. The bird was mature but relatively young—under five years old. By noon on Monday, he had abandoned all other vocalizations and was driving his very favorite human crazy with LOUD cockatiel shrieks.

Feather obviously doted on his "Dad," a retired businessman who lived alone in a downtown skyscraper. He was really quite interested to see a stranger willing to put a gray towel over her head and hide behind corners, magazines, plants, and the ends of the towel to play peek-a-boo.

Although Feather had been shrieking almost constantly from the time I stepped off the elevator, within one minute of beginning an intense game of peek-a-boo, he was totally quiet, mesmerized by this odd human behavior. Within 15 minutes, he was calling out trial words like *"Hello"* and *"What?"* in an effort to participate in the game. By the next morning, Feather had figured out how to say *"Peek-a-boo,"* and for a few days, replaced all vocalizations with that one, very exciting, phrase.

Because we worked on the newly acquired behavior immediately and very dramatically, our efforts were completely successful. Feather never again shrieked like a cockatiel, but rather tries, whenever possible, to engage willing humans in peeking games. (Barron's *African Grey Parrot Handbook* by Mattie Sue Athan and Dianalee Deter.)

Attention-Demanding Vocalizations

The most usual source of complaints regarding "screaming" involves attention-demanding vocalizations. Young parrots can be extremely adept at demanding attention. After all, it is how they survived as neonates—they made a lot of noise and got their parents to feed them.

Attention-demanding vocalizations develop readily if a young bird learns that if it makes more obnoxious noises, it gets more attention. A companion parrot's ability to play independently greatly influences the nature of vocal behaviors that develop. From the moment a baby parrot is aware of its surroundings, interesting tools (toys) must be provided to generate self-rewarding play behaviors. If a parrot does not learn to amuse itself, if it doesn't have easy access to alternative behaviors, no amount of ignoring of the screaming in the other room will improve the bird's behavior.

Not all loud vocalizations can be eliminated. Early morning and evening calls seem important and irreplaceable. Many birds feel they must scream when anybody comes home—friend, foe, or stranger.

Screaming must be dealt with patiently, compassionately, and sympathetically, for it does have a purpose. If your bird is screaming excessively, then something is wrong. It is a good idea to seek immediate professional help, for parrot volume can be most easily turned down if annoying new vocalizations are addressed quickly. Behavioral programs are usually designed to replace the unwanted vocalizations with different behaviors. Sometimes those replacement behaviors are other vocalizations; sometimes they are simply different behaviors such as chewing, playing, bathing, or napping.

The Bird That Damages Feathers

Sameness is stressful for a parrot. In human terms that means that life in one room can be maddeningly boring for a creature that is genetically programmed to live and reproduce in a wild and challenging world. Like a bored student chewing on a cuticle in a long lecture, it's only natural for a confined, chewing-motivated parrot to preen, and overpreening can develop into habitual damaging of the feathers. But feather picking might be related to many things other than boredom. Sometimes it's just a habit—one

of those behaviors that was accidentally rewarded.

Feather-damaging behavior can appear suddenly in minutes or hours or can take months, even years, to be noticeable. As soon as you are aware of it, look for medical advice. Don't wait; go quickly to the avian veterinarian before the behavior becomes habitual. Treating a medical condition will often resolve a feather-damaging incident. If, however, feather chewing remains after medical issues are resolved, then consider diet or habitat manipulation and/or behavior counseling.

Presuming no medical issues, a juvenile parrot pulling, snapping, or chewing off dirty or damaged feathers should be bathed more often, exercised more often, and monitored carefully. Toys and other entertainments must

Stress-related feather damaging behaviors can appear suddenly or develop slowly over months or years.

be easily accessible. Be careful to reinforce only those behaviors you want to see again and not reinforce feather-damaging behaviors that are sometimes done for attention.

Sensitivities and Diet
Investigate the possibility of fumes, food, or other sensitivities when feather-damaging behaviors appear. Occasionally, radical adjustment of the diet must be made, possibly removing all but one food, then gradually adding foods to observe their effect. Sometimes, eliminating salt, corn, grapes, or peanuts and improving protein, calcium, vitamin A, and/or

iodine-rich foods helps. Don't supplement vitamins without a veterinarian's supervision.

Self-inflicted damage to the skin is not, usually, a behavioral issue. Any parrot chewing skin, especially if blood is involved, requires immediate veterinary attention. Self-mutilation is sometimes traced to airborne toxins such as pesticides, solvents, or cigarette smoke.

Collars

Collars or other devices are temporary means of preventing damage. Combined with improved behavioral practice, they are sometimes necessary and often beneficial. Some chewing-prevention devices have a built-in toy called a "teaser" that deflects the bird's beak to a more appropriate chewable substance. If the parrot has not learned replacement behavior, or the issues behind the plucking are not resolved, the bird will resume plucking when the collar is removed.

Controlling Feather-Damaging Behaviors

✔ If feather-damaging behaviors appear suddenly, examine the environment for things that might be causing stress.

✔ Look for new things that might represent frightening change to the bird such as new art, light fixtures, carpeting, or sound-producing clocks.

✔ Consider the possibility that a human or another companion animal might be secretly provoking the bird.

✔ Examine the cage for appropriate elements, such as size, color (some birds are sensitive to

A collar may be necessary to limit damage in extreme cases.

some colors, especially black), and location (a corner, no window), destructible perches, and toys. Toys should be easily accessible, hanging beside rather than under the bird.

✔ Check to see that perches are not too large, too smooth, or too hard. Safe, nontoxic chewable toys and branches, offered in various sizes and textures, provide necessary opportunities for decision making, developing dexterity, chewing, snuggling, talking, masturbating, and dominating—all elements that stimulate curiosity and eliminate the stress of boredom.

✔ Exercise is a significant part of a wild parrot's life. Lack of exercise can result in the bird's metabolism gradually slowing down. Sedentary birds are more likely to chew feathers.

✔ Bathing functions as exercise for companion birds, especially in birds that don't use their wings much. Most parrots need a bath at least

a couple of times weekly. Most can be stimulated to bathe in the water bowl by turning up the thermostat and providing a fine mist of cool water from a bottle. Allowing the bird to dry naturally, even though it might shiver just a bit, provides similar metabolic and vascular benefits to flapping and climbing exercise. Frequent showers also assist in the completion of molting and remove dirt that interferes with preening.

✔ Work on improving a bird's confidence. That means raising the confidence of some birds, and lowering that of others. Some birds feel safer housed behind a plant or other visual barrier. Many birds benefit from having places to hide. This might mean covering the top of the cage with a towel or providing a small enclosure for hiding and peeking out.

✔ Inappropriate wing and nail grooming can contribute to self-inflicted feather damage just as correcting grooming can assist in recovery. Too short nails can contribute to falling; nails that are too long might get caught in fabric or in cage parts, causing stress as the bird moves around. A ragged or too short wing feather trim can contribute to falls and to preening disorders. Some birds recover from feather-damaging behaviors when wing feathers are allowed to grow out completely, then are trimmed only slightly after the bird learns or relearns to fly.

✔ Keep a journal to determine exactly what's going on when a bird is chewing feathers. Note human reactions. Humans must provide for, stimulate, and reinforce other appropriate behaviors. Be sure there are many ways for the bird to communicate what it needs, either with words or actions. A bird that is frustrated by unmet needs may turn to feather picking or screaming.

Owning a feather-chewing parrot is not unlike having a teenager with a habit of nail biting or a fascination with tattoos or piercings. We can't withhold love from a beloved human or bird merely because we don't approve of that individual's personal grooming or ornamentation tastes. A feather-chewing companion parrot is no more likely to be neurotic or unhappy than a human who chews fingernails. Often, it's just a habit. Nothing more, nothing less.

Behavior Training: When and Where to Find Help

Your bird Lolita has decided not allow your husband into the house, and he is getting more and more willing to stay away. The bird won't let you out of her sight without self-destructing and telling the whole neighborhood about it. You've read every book you can find, and she still has you wrapped around a slightly overgrown toenail.

It is not unusual for mere humans to be very anxious about asking someone into their homes to help with their bird's behavior. Could this sort of thing be a painful and intimate experience like psychoanalysis? Where do humans get help with bird behavior problems, and what can they expect when they do?

The basis of all behavior modification involves the replacement of one behavior with another. An effective parrot behavior consultant probably works something like a coach, advising strategies for stimulating and reinforcing planned behaviors. A good behavior consultant deals compassionately with the bird and with the humans who care for the bird.

Of course, in order to change the bird's behavior, one must have an understanding of the forces that stimulated and reinforced the behavior into patterns. In this way distractions and more pleasing patterns can be planned for, stimulated, and reinforced.

The Bird Behavior Consultant

✔ Your favorite breeder, bird store, or avian veterinarian should be able to refer you to a parrot behavior consultant in your area. If they are unfamiliar with a local working in the field, they might recommend telephone counseling. Try looking at the behavior consultant ads in the back of your favorite bird magazine.

✔ There are quite a few behavioral alternatives on the Internet. Some are wonderful; some are awful. Look for places where kindness and open minds prevail.

✔ Ask for references from people who have actually spoken with a particular consultant about a similar problem in a similar type of bird. Watch out for someone who seems to know everything, but who offers that advice at no charge. Don't be offended if a professional expects to be paid for his or her time. Sometimes you get a bargain; sometimes you get what you pay for.

✔ Expect an initial screening consultation by telephone. Before making an appointment, a parrot behavior consultant will want to know the age, source, type of bird, nature, and duration of the problem. You may then expect a description of what kind of expenditure of time and money might be needed in order to resolve the issue. A professional will also be evaluating your responses and trying to determine whether or not the two of you have a rapport. Expect to be referred to another consultant if either of you don't feel a good emotional connection.

✔ The consultant might offer group, telephone, or in-home counseling depending upon the location and nature of the problem. Group work must be done very carefully because even very healthy-looking birds might be carrying undiagnosed or contagious disease. Telephone counseling is attractive and more and more common, but in-home evaluation may be necessary to solve long-term, enduring problems. While in-home counseling might appear more expensive at the outset, it probably offers greater opportunity for success, as sometimes only direct observation by an outsider can reveal what is happening to perpetuate a behavior. In the long run, one-on-one, in-home counseling is usually the most cost-effective option for correcting established behavior problems in companion parrots.

✔ The bird behavior consultant will be looking for environmental elements such as diet, housing, and experiences with humans that might be contributing to the bird's behavior. The consultant will be looking for indications of typical interactions between the bird and other family members as well as making observations about how the bird is responding with this unfamiliar person in the home. The bird is often perfectly behaved during the in-home counseling. This is a good sign. It lets the humans in the home see how much control the bird has over its own behavior.

✔ Most in-home services will probably include grooming or towel play with the bird in order to observe the bird's responses. This can ultimately save the bird's life, for a bird that responds poorly to the towel is existing in a life-threatening state.

✔ A good behavior consultant might never even touch the bird, especially if the bird is shy. Handling may not be an option. Especially in cases involving shyness or fearfulness, expect the behaviorist to offer suggestions regarding adjusting the bird's behavior through making changes in the environment. Environmental

An Amazon might be an extremely vigorous bather.

enrichment is usually the easiest, most direct, and most effective way to change bird behavior.

✔ The behavioral consultant might want to observe feather condition and the bird's responses to showering. The easiest way to do this, of course is to give the bird a bath as a part of the behavioral evaluation. It is not unusual for the consultation to wind up in a waterproof room such as the bathroom. You might want to tidy up a bit if you are shy about strangers in the bathroom, although, a real pro won't care whether the bathroom is sparkling clean, and certainly would protect this confidence, anyway.

✔ Expect some basic information on the role of diet in behavior. Missing, unnecessary, or

Bird clubs can be a wonderful resource for parrot behavior information.

Parrot behavior training can often be accessed through seminars and conferences as well as through private in-home consultations.

empty unfulfilling nutrition can affect a bird's behavior, and changing diet can change behavior (see Barron's *Feeding Your Pet Bird* by Petra Burgmann).

✔ Expect a responsible companion bird behavior consultant to refer you to an appropriate avian veterinarian if there is a suspicion that health issues may affect the case.

✔ Expect to enjoy the interaction and to have your life touched in a significant way. It is not unusual for family members to weep with joy when they make a major breakthrough in the rehabilitation of a problem behavior. It is important to like and to trust the professionals who work with your bird; your life and your bird's life may be changed from this day on.

below: A parrot enjoys a snack.

Note: Any parrot that lives more than a couple of decades will probably have to survive some type of household emergency at least once in its lifetime. Because they are genetically programmed to fight or flee when danger threatens, caged birds can suffer on-going "psychological" or behavioral damage from being exposed to very frightening circumstances. Keep the carrier covered when chaos reigns. Keep the bird as calm, warm, and quiet as possible.

Inhaled Toxins

No matter what the actual emergency unfolding, the first greatest danger to indoor birds is inhaled toxins. Carbon monoxide or other fumes from even insignificant-seeming events can kill indoor birds before they affect anyone or anything else. Parrots can succumb quickly due to the sensitivity of their extensive respiratory systems.

If you suspect that any synthetic fiber or plastic has been heated sufficiently to release fumes—whether or not it is actually burning—remove all birds immediately. Even if it is not overheated, polytetrafluoroethylene, sometimes called Teflon, any burning plastics—mini blinds, plastic bottles, carpeting, or chemicals—produce fumes that can kill a parrot.

Modern home smoke and carbon monoxide detectors are necessary and proper in bird homes, but unusual bird behavior can be the first clue that something out of the ordinary is going on. Earthquakes, unseen, smoldering fires, and intruders into the home are commonly signaled by vocalizations or other behaviors by companion parrots.

In Case of an Emergency

✔ Evacuation first, is the first rule of fire safety. While it might seem prudent to grab the fire extinguisher first, if there are birds in the home, the birds are more likely to survive if you evacuate first and fight the fire second. Even professional firefighters evacuate first, and it is helpful for them to know how many animals need to be removed before they can begin fighting the fire. For this reason, there should be an indication of the number and type of animal inhabitants posted near the front door. There are stickers available at your favorite pet supply store to easily provide this information. Transportation or release instructions should be visible near each cage.

Remove all birds as quickly as possible from any source of toxic fumes.

✔ Keep an appropriate carrier (or at least a pillowcase) within reach of the bird's cage so that the bird can be removed quickly. The carrier should be clean and with lots of extra newspaper. It is a good idea to already have a closed container of food and a sealed bottle of water inside as well as a towel in case it is cold or smoky and you need to cover the carrier. Have a sticker with your name and address and an emergency phone number as well as your veterinarian's phone number permanently attached to the carrier.

✔ If there is no easy way to transport the bird to safety, sometimes it might be preferable to release the bird, maybe gently lofting it toward a nearby tree or other rooftop, then worry about recapturing it later. This is not ideal, of course, but a flying bird can be recovered; a dead bird cannot. A bird that has spent time in an outdoor cage or flight is more likely to stay close by and be more easily recovered after danger passes.

✔ If the bird won't come out of the cage, and the cage is too large to carry out, take the dishes and tray out and turn the cage on its back or upside down. Almost all birds will then climb immediately out of the cage and can be toweled and put into the hard-sided emergency carrier.

Weather Emergencies

In weather emergencies—blizzards, tornadoes, hurricanes—don't be overly concerned with immediately generating heat. Many alternative heat sources such as propane or kerosene stoves produce toxic fumes, and birds are generally more endangered by fumes than they are by cold. A healthy bird that is dry and pro-

Always have a first aid kit ready.

tected from wind can handle a little cold, even a day or two of subfreezing temperatures. Provide warm food, if possible, oatmeal or pasta, and keep the cage mostly covered.

Disasters

In disasters that threaten a building's structure, seek shelter from falling walls and flying debris. Take the bird or birds in rigid carriers with you into the bathtub and cover yourself and your birds with a mattress (be sure to leave a way for oxygen to get in).

If water supplies are threatened, store at least a two-week supply of fresh water. Always keep at least a two-week supply of the bird's basic diet in the freezer so that if there is a disaster just as the bird's food is depleted, the bird does not wind up living on cereal for a month, although, in an on-going emergency, unsweetened human cereal can keep a stranded companion bird alive for a few weeks or even more.

LIFESTYLE ISSUES

It is easy to think of a long-time companion parrot as a member of the family, but the fact remains that a parrot is a bird and related issues will continue to present themselves in the human/avian family. Once you get the hang of day-to-day needs, you will still occasionally run into a few situations that most people would not anticipate.

Traveling: To Take the Bird or Leave It Behind

Most humans don't have the luxury of allowing their birds to accompany them to work, and traveling with parrots can be difficult and dangerous. So who takes care of the bird when you can't be there? A well-informed parrot keeper also knows exactly how to plan for the unique problem of retrieving a friend who flies, a bird's specialized medical needs, disaster situations, and parrots' incredibly long potential life spans.

Travel by car or motor home is probably the most comfortable for human/parrot vacations, but a loose bird in the vehicle could be a distraction and safety hazard to the driver and everybody else on the road. The bird travels best—safely and happily—in the hard-sided carrier strapped in with a seat belt. Once you

A tame parrot can find lots of ways to get into trouble.

arrive at your destination, the bird can be housed in the roost cage or in a folding travel cage that it has been acclimated to before the trip.

Airline travel is more difficult. Federal Aviation Association rules require that only one pet carrier be on each passenger flight. The bird/pet must fit into a carrier that will fit under the airline seat, or it will wind up in cargo, and conditions in cargo simply aren't reliable or consistent enough to be safe for a bird. If you are crossing state lines, the bird must have a health certificate.

Be sure the bird's wings are trimmed. Even though it will be in a carrier most of the time, you will probably be required to remove it so that the carrier can be examined when you pass through security checkpoints.

Many airlines have very severe restrictions on traveling with companion animals. Be sure to make a reservation. International travel is especially complicated, and sometimes impossible, as many limitations exist when trying to take parrots from one country to another.

To Board or Not to Board

As editor of *Positively Pets*, a highly visible city pet tabloid, I receive at least one tragic call monthly (more in January) about companion animals that had become ill, had been injured, or died as a result of uncompensated or unprofessional pet-sitters. The needs of companion parrots are so specialized that it may be necessary to place them in a boarding facility if you can't find a qualified in-home pet-sitter.

In-home Pet-sitting

In-home pet-sitting is probably best for companion parrots, especially if the bird is very sensitive or if there are many parrots and/or other companion animals. Familiar surroundings with many familiar elements such as familiar water, familiar food, music, television, or video movies can enhance the bird's sense of security and keep the bird on a happy behavioral track until you get home.

A pet-sitter with parrot experience is not always easy to find, however, especially in rural areas. Start looking at the avian veterinarian's office. Many veterinarian's technicians do specialty pet-sitting in off hours or know someone who does. If you can't find a pet-sitter with bird experience, ask around for a dependable pet-sitter with impeccable references who is willing to learn bird care.

Boarding

Boarding is better than nonprofessional pet-sitters, but it is not ideal. The bird could come home with unwanted behaviors copied from other birds or learned as a result of being inadvertently reinforced. A healthy, human-bonded bird in unfamiliar surroundings, especially, needs more human attention when it is left in a boarding facility than when it is left at home.

Bad behavior is probably easier to pick up than illness, but illness is also a possibility. Look for a facility with good hygiene practices and cleaning staff members that interact sensitively with their charges. A busy avian veterinarian's facility may be the best choice. If you hear music and see someone disinfecting cages and talking or singing to the animals in adjacent cages, then you have probably found a good place.

Preventing Feelings of Abandonment

Behavioral complications can result if a well-bonded companion parrot is unprepared for the first separation from its human flock. Sudden disappearance of the flock could mean death in nature. Screaming or fearfulness can develop, but feather chewing is probably the most common issue to appear in companion parrots when first experiencing abandonment, especially during the long winter holidays.

Birds need to understand that when you go away, you will come back. This concept is even important when humans work long hours outside the home. If the bird must spend the day alone, then the environment must be planned to facilitate independent activities, feelings of safety, and ways for the bird to know that time is passing.

Establish a pattern of going away and coming back. This can be done gradually, with the new baby being left for an hour or two at first, then for longer and longer periods before leaving it alone all day. Before leaving your parrot alone for a weekend, leave it alone for one night, and before leaving it alone for a week, leave it alone for a weekend (with a qualified pet-sitter, of course). This is a good way to acclimate the bird to the regular coming and going of the pet-sitter, who should come every day at the same time.

Counting

I believe that every bird should learn elementary counting skills. This is more feasible with larger than smaller birds, however, and more necessary with larger than smaller birds. This can be accomplished in much the same way that human children learn to count: Just count when you give them things.

Be sure to provide some mechanism for the bird to understand when you will come back. Chris Davis suggests counting out the number of days to be gone on the fingers. However any simple system that the bird is familiar with will achieve the desired result.

For example, a when-Mom/Dad-comes-back association might be formed this way: When you're going to be gone for one night, leave one toy (now called the "last" toy) out in plain view; then give it to the bird the next day when you return. When you are to be gone two nights, leave two toys out, having the pet-sitter give the first toy on the first day and you give the last toy when you return the second day. Then, when you are gone for a longer time, leave a toy for each day you are to be gone. Have the pet-sitter give the bird one toy each day, and when that last toy is the only one left, a bird that has experienced it before will instinctively perceive that you will be home in time to give him the last toy. Try to use the same toy as the last toy every time, if that is possible.

I Need a Peach-faced Lovebird!

"It has to have yellow patches on its wings," a man's voice on the phone announced.

I was filling in at my favorite bird store when the manager took a vacation between Christmas and New Year's.

"Well, I've got one with no yellow on the wings that's a total doll baby and loves everybody, and that's just ready to go to a new home."

"That won't do!" the man screamed and slammed the phone down.

An hour later, the same voice on the other end of the line was adamant, again, that we should "keep looking for a lovebird with yellow patches on the wings."

Then he decided to come clean.

"I was watching my daughter's lovebird over the holidays. She told me that it had to have food and water every day, but when I looked in the bowls, it always seemed like there was food and water there, so I didn't add any. This morning when I found the bird dead, I realized that the powder in the bowl was leftovers and that the bird hadn't eaten in days. My family comes home tomorrow."

The grieving father did come in for the darling peach-faced lovebird, but he had to tell his family what he had done. I'm sure it wasn't easy.

Radio or Television

If you're gone for long periods during the day, consider setting a radio or television to come on for an hour or two, then go off, midafternoon. This adds a little variety to your parrot's life without annoying him with sound all day. It provides a sense of transition.

Perceiving the Passage of Time

A bird inhabiting a controlled environment might never see shadows grow long then short then long, or hear routine sounds of nature that occur at the same time every day. An indoor bird never knows the heat of the noonday sun followed by cooling afternoon rain. During my in-home evaluations, I am often entertained with stories of birds that stare at the clock for 10 or 20 minutes before Mom/Dad gets home from work or birds that start screaming 30 seconds before the car turns up the block for home in the evening.

I believe a bird that has an opportunity to easily perceive the passage of time is not as likely to self-mutilate or demand attention because it is familiar with what is going on. Easily understandable signals that time is passing provide a sense of safety; ritualized interactions ensure that there will be no surprises. Look for any kind of environmental elements, a chiming clock or cuckoo clock, that can

A lost companion parrot is vulnerable to many outdoor dangers.

demonstrate the passage of time. My own birds love clocks that feature a different song bird every hour; they know exactly what time it is every daylight hour.

To Fly or Not to Fly

You only have to see one bird die an agonizing death from flying into hot cooking oil or find one drowned in the toilet to become absolutely sputteringly militant on the topic of wing trims. But trimmed wings aren't behaviorally healthy for every companion bird. Allowing wing feathers to regrow is an important part of behavioral strategy for the treatment of such things as failure of curiosity, being picked on by another bird or pet, or the self-destruction of feathers. Additionally, birds with bad or missing legs or feet benefit from being allowed flight. This is especially appropriate if the bird has a weight problem or has developed depressed or sedentary behavior.

Of course, *human responsibilities* are greatly increased when there's a flighted bird in the home. The home must be carefully modified for safety (see Hazards in the Home, page 26). There can never be open standing water: no uncovered toilets, no mop buckets, no kitchen sinks. The bird must be contained whenever there is cooking or live fireplace maintenance. Ceiling fans must be caged or skirted. Areas the bird will have access to should be examined for potentially toxic substances such as candles, incense, room deodorant, live plants, and stained glass or other sources of lead.

Birds that are allowed flight must also be protected from flying away, so it is best to have two doors between the inside and the outside of the home. Enclosed porches or mud rooms safeguard birds from accidental flyaways and save energy.

For better or worse, a companion parrot's life is completely dependent upon the meticulousness and judgment of humans. Only the humans involved have truly informed consent; the birds don't have a clue how dangerous either outdoor or indoor flight can be. But humans are, well, only human, and there will always be humans who believe that a bird should spend its life flying, no matter how many veterinarians, breeders, behavior consultants, groomers, and recapture technicians say otherwise. Whether or not a companion bird is kept flighted is ultimately the decision of the human who cares for that bird. It is not a decision to be taken lightly.

In-home pet sitting is preferable when there are many companion animals in the home.

The price for that flying "quality of life" could be death. Could you live with yourself if your bird was injured as a result of your carelessness or your decision not to trim wing feathers?

Refledging

It is good for the bird's health and general well-being if it is allowed at least a little flight every spring before wings are trimmed for the summer open-door-and-window season. This can be done gradually as wing feathers regrow during molting. As you see increased experimental use of wings, you can encourage a little flight by gently lofting the bird toward the middle of a large, soft bed, and later allow the bird to fly a few feet back to the cage from the perch when it is time to eat. If the bird is

The Survivors

Gail Langsner, a bird trainer, lived in the shadow of the World Trade Center for 22 years. She remembered the bombing of 1993, but nothing prepared her for the events of September 11, 2001. In an Associated Press story by Helen O'Neill, Langsner relates how she and her boyfriend, Nate Priest escaped with the birds from the ash and burning debris when the buildings came down.

When the second plane hit the South Tower, Gail and Nate bundled the seven birds—Aristotle and Peter, the Grey parrots; Josie, the blue-and-gold macaw; Jonquil, the red-lored Amazon; Caesar, the Hahn's macaw; Echo, the Senegal; and Fez, the half-moon conure, into smaller cages and rushed to the more-sheltered apartment of a neighbor. Crouched in the corner in a back room with a sheet over the birds, they huddled together with their neighbors and their dogs while the unimaginable was made real. First one tower and then the other collapsed in flames to the streets below. In the suffocating aftermath, black smoke and small fires began to consume the world around them. The birds were trembling, matted, and dirty, but they were alive.

Nate improvised a broom handle to carry the large cages himself. Gail put the smaller birds into duffle bags, and their neighbors carried their dogs out. They wrapped towels around their faces and made their way through the dust and the flames with the masses of other dazed survivors. Gail used her cell phone to notify her family that she was OK. Separating from their neighbors, they turned west, sometimes backtracking to go around areas blocked by debris as they made their way toward the Hudson River.

Occasionally, they heard Peter, the African Grey's, muffled, plaintive *"Hello."* It was their only indication that the birds were alive. As they fought for breaths in the filthy air and hiked toward safety, there was no thought of life or death, just moment, by moment, one-breath-at-a-time survival.

Yes, they made it out, but the birds may have some long-term physical damage. Gail and Nate have their own kind of injury: They have to live with their memories. Five months later, Gail says, "Maybe we'll always be haunted."

hungry, this happens automatically. Start by placing the perch next to the cage, then gradually increase the distance between the two.

If the decision has been made to allow the bird to retain flight capability, safety measures should be in place. The environment must be modified as previously discussed. Additionally, companion birds that are allowed full wings should be trained to fly dependably to humans upon request. This must be done indoors and is best accomplished during the time the bird is learning to fly again. The most dependable early response will be if the person the bird is flying to is the highest thing in the immediate area. Start by requesting that the bird step-up to your hand, then encourage short hops to the hand, then longer jumps that will eventually require flight.

Over the Rainbow: Going After the Bird That Flies Away

There was a time when novice birdkeepers might just say, "Oh, well," if their bird flew away. There was a time when people seemed to think that a bird just automatically died when it escaped. Experienced parrot owners now know that a companion parrot can usually survive outdoors, but sometimes at great cost. The wilds of a city are fraught with danger for an ill-prepared animal, and when a bird flies away from one place, it goes to another place. It is all just a matter of figuring out where the bird went and going after it.

When a companion parrot flies away, try to keep the bird in sight, or within the sound of your voice. Sometimes an athletic whistle can be helpful in maintaining sound contact.

Act quickly to recover the bird before it learns to forage on its own. It usually takes at least a few days for a normal companion parrot to figure out where to find food and water. Within 48 hours, a lost hand-fed, domestic bird should be hungry and thirsty and should come willingly to almost anyone. If you're there, the bird will come to you.

If wing feathers have been trimmed, it's important to recover the bird before additional wing feathers regrow. Sometimes only *one* primary flight feather on one wing can enable a previously grounded bird to fly. Many parrots fly at dawn and dusk and not much in between. These "flight times" are a prime time for recovery.

Flying Down

Most birds—particularly larger ones that are unaccustomed to flying—might not quite comprehend flying down. When coaxing a bird to fly down remember to have the wind at your back when you are looking at the bird. The bird must be supported by air pushing up under its wings. If there is wind, the bird must, essentially, jump into the wind and cannot take off with the wind coming from behind the wings.

Climbing Down

✔ A bird that is not an accomplished flyer is best *lured* to climb down. Climb as far up the tree as you can easily. Since electrocution is a great danger, carefully position yourself so that neither you, the ladder, nor the bird will come into contact with power lines. A bird can survive a walk on a live wire if it is not grounded or connected to the ground, but be sure to stay out of reach as long as the bird is on the wire, in case the bird grabs for you and you happen to be grounded.

✔ Try to have a little family group on the ground (containing both loved and hated members of the bird's immediate social group), noisily and delightedly eating foods that the bird likes. Be eating something yourself, crunching and chewing loudly. Tap on the trunk or branch of the tree so that the bird can feel the vibrations and lure the bird to you by describing how yummy that food is.

✔ Some parrots can be lured down with food and some can be lured down with a like bird, but jealousy is a much more dependable lure. A bird that is extremely bonded to the owner can often be stimulated to come down immediately to express jealousy against a known or perceived rival for the attentions of the bird's favorite person.

✔ If you are lucky, you will have to climb down with a possibly angry bird. If so, stick a

Lories are great fliers and famous escape artists.

Sometimes you have to rent heavy equipment to get to a lost bird.

Excessive vocalizations and feather damage are the most common complications of separation anxiety.

Sometimes recovering a flown-away parrot is as simple as walking over and saying "step-up."

The veterinarian can teach you to do your own bird's nails.

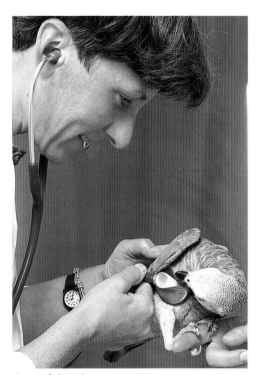

A careful and conscientious veterinarian can ensure your bird's long life.

Who will take care of your bird when you can't do it anymore?

A companion parrot can find lots of mischief when left unsupervised.

pillowcase and a bit of the bird's favorite food in your pocket before you climb. You may have only one chance. Make the most of it. If you do get your hand on the bird, do not let go! You might get a bruise, you might bleed a little, but the odds of having a bone broken by the bite are remote. Put the bird inside the pillowcase and tie it closed with a self-locking cable tie or a piece of twine. Then pass or drop the pillowcase to a helper below so that you don't have to climb down with the bird.

Note: Don't try to use a water hose to get the bird so wet that it can't fly. This rarely works and can leave a wet bird sitting out in the cold. On the other hand, those long-range water guns are excellent for "herding" a bird to more and more accessible locations. Aim above the bird or at its tail and try to get it to fly to lower and lower perches.

Borrowing or Renting Equipment

If you must enter someone else's property or borrow equipment such as a ladder, scaffold, or rope, or if you have to hire a cherry picker, you may be asked to release the owner from liability related to the bird recapture. This must be done in writing in a manner that will assure all other parties that you and your heirs will not hold anyone responsible for damages of any kind, and that you will, in fact, be responsible for any damages done in the process of recapturing the bird. If someone else is going to climb the tree for you, talk about safety in advance and discuss who would be liable if the human climber is injured, or the bird is accidentally injured.

An equipment rental company or a tree service company might be willing to rent equipment to reach the bird. Some fire departments will help; some will not. At least a bird-at-large situation is not yet (usually) punished with a summons and fine.

Trapping

Birds that have already learned to find food and water on their own must often be trapped. Begin by feeding the bird at a location where it has been seen to eat, then gradually move the food source inside a cage with a remote door-closure mechanism. Or lure the bird with a like species friend confined in a small cage inside a larger cage/trap.

Fliers

If you've lost track of the bird, treat the matter as a public relations project. Notify animal control. File a report of "missing property" with police so that if someone has your bird and won't give it up, police will be able to help you access the steps necessary to retrieve your bird. This is a good case for DNA registry or microchipping identification systems.

✔ Make an attractive flier featuring a picture of a parrot of the type that is missing or of the actual bird. Send or fax the flier to every bird-related business or organization within a 30-mile (48 km) area.

✔ The flier should include a contact phone number (preferably a mobile number since you will be out looking for the bird) and the street corner or local landmark where the bird was last seen.

✔ It should mention small rewards for information leading to the bird and a "sizable" reward for the bird's return. Most people will refuse a reward anyway rather than have to take care of an unfamiliar creature that has accidentally flown into their garage.

Thank Heaven for Towels

At 60, Ruth Machlachlan was a retired divorcee, who loved the company of lories. She lived in a ground-level condo with Heckle and Jeckle, two blue-streaked lories, and a rainbow lorikeet named Joseph. Every morning Ruth had breakfast and read the paper while the lories pinned their eyes and squealed with delight as they squashed the juices out of fruit and vegetable pieces and soaked what remained in their water bowls.

Then Heckle and Jeckle got a bowl of water with ice cubes to play in while Ruth and Joseph retired to the bathroom for the morning shower ritual. Joseph pranced up and down, back and forth across the square top of the shower stall while Ruth washed her hair and splashed water for the brightly colored, pinning, squealing, and posturing bird.

One morning, the newspaper was late and the whole crew did the eating and shower ritual before the paper came. At about 6:30 A.M., when she heard the thud at the doorstep, Ruth went to retrieve the newspaper. Wrapping her naked body in a towel, she set Joseph down on a perch in the living room. But when she stooped to pick up the newspaper, she saw a flash of color over her head, and Joseph landed on the sidewalk about a dozen feet away from her. Without a thought about it, Ruth pulled the towel from her body, stepped out into the large communal courtyard, tossed the towel over Joseph, scooped him up, and rushed inside.

Over the course of the next few weeks, Ruth realized that she always had help carrying her groceries in. Teenagers in the neighborhood seemed much friendlier. By the end of the summer, Ruth was hearing that one neighbor's son was saying that she had "a pretty good bod for an old bat."

✔ Be sure to mention identifying characteristics such as a missing toe or banding on a particular leg. If the bird has a band, don't reveal the number so that the information can be used to differentiate between a person who really has your bird and an unscrupulous one who might be pretending to have it.

✔ Most people will be honest and helpful. Talk with everyone you see, and post copies of your flier on brightly colored paper around town.

✔ Many cities now have code enforcement staff to make sure people don't post signs on traffic and utility poles. There might be a fine for posting fliers; however, if yours contains the following line: "This notice will be removed *promptly* when the bird is found," a sympathetic code enforcement officer might humanely look the other way for a few hours until the bird is found. Then, when the bird is found, be sure to take the fliers down *promptly* or face a fine.

✔ A better plan might be to stop by the hardware store and pick up a bundle of wooden stakes, then post the fliers like election campaign signs staked in the grass. Regardless of how they are posted, prompt removal of the signs will signal the neighbors that they don't have to keep looking for the bird.

A parrot inspects its claw.

A parrot rests precariously on a branch.

When You Find Your Bird

Keep looking. Pace yourself. Get as much rest and good food as possible. Don't give up, even if the weather is below freezing. The bird is not going to die just because it spent the night out in the cold. Whether it's a long time or a short time until it is recovered, the bird might come home sick or injured. You may need to be strong for nursing it back to health.

When you find the bird, it will probably be hungry and thirsty. Don't let the bird drink too much too fast. It should want to empty the food bowl more than once. If the bird is weak or was outside wet in cold weather, take it immediately to an avian veterinarian. Provide Pedialyte or Lactated Ringers or Gatorade (if it's all you have) for a possibly dehydrated bird. Some veterinarians are available for emergency counseling during this ordeal and will meet you at the clinic if a sick bird is found outside office hours.

Don't give up. Anyone who works in the field of bird recapture can tell you that there are usually more companion birds found than are reported lost. If you act quickly, there's an excellent chance of success. More than half of the flyaways reported to me are retrieved within the first 24 hours.

You, Your Bird, and the Veterinarian

The relationship with the veterinarian can be the bird's most significant relationship outside the family. Amazing advances in avian medicine have been made in the last two decades. A sick bird isn't, necessarily a dead bird, although size can be a factor here. A small bird such as a budgie, lovebird, or lory reaches a crisis point more quickly than a large one.

Starting with a well-baby check, keep the bird's records together. If you move from one city to another, be sure to have the records moved. Here's where the record of those early tests can save a bird's life.

A companion parrot might experience illness and have more than one serious medical emergency in its long, long, lifetime—or a bird might have only one serious emergency and a short life. Access to quality veterinary care has seen my own Amazon, Portia, through four serious medical issues in her twenty-five years. An imported bird, he was treated for two episodes of psittacosis before he was five, then survived a gram-negative infection when he was eighteen. He has fought a weight problem since he was ten, and I nearly lost him to complications related to his weight this year. It was very, very scary, and a couple of times he was flat on the bottom of the carrier. I did not see how he could possibly survive, but five days after he nearly died in it, Portia explored the carrier beside his cage as a potential nest site. By that time, he was obviously feeling well enough to consider starting a family.

If you see a behavior change, especially if that behavior change involves eating or drinking (or not), put the bird into a carrier, keep it warm and quiet, and get it immediately to the avian veterinarian. The sooner you get there, the more likely the bird will survive. If your bird likes a particular towel of a particular color, be sure to take that towel with you so that the veterinarian's examination will seem less scary to the bird. Most birds appear to feel safer if their eyes can be covered during the examination, especially if they are being manipulated and turned quickly. Squeamish humans might have to cover their own eyes when blood is drawn, but most birds probably feel safer if you stay in the room with them.

After You're Gone

Whether we lose the ability to care for a bird because of illness, death, or changing life circumstances, the reality of caring for a long-lived species is that sometimes the bird lives longer than our ability to care for it. This is another one of those wonderful advantages of smaller species: Humans have a good chance to outlive them. If you're getting along in years or otherwise become unable to care for your bird, see Barron's *The Second-hand Parrot* for detailed information about finding and evaluating a new home for a parrot.

If you're old enough to have a parrot, you're old enough to have a will. And if you have a parrot, the bird must be named and described in the will. It is best to find more than one person who is willing to take care of your bird when you're gone, just in case you happen to outlive the person you chose as parrot guardian.

If you have more than one large bird, it is also best to leave a trust fund for the birds' care. If you've read this far in this book, you know that parrots are a big responsibility and that involves both time and money. Even if it has not been possible for you to designate a specific caretaker for your birds, you can establish a trust fund for their care and appoint an unrelated trustee to oversee the trust fund. You will be comfortable knowing that you have seen things through to the end, that you have done your best by your bird.

Useful Literature

Athan, Mattie Sue. *Guide to a Well-Behaved Parrot.* Hauppauge, NY: Barron's Educational Series, Inc., 1999.

Athan, Mattie Sue. *Guide to Companion Parrot Behavior.* Hauppauge, NY: Barron's Educational Series, Inc., 1999.

Athan, Mattie Sue and Deter, Dianalee. *Guide to the Senegal Parrot and Its Family.* Hauppauge, NY: Barron's Educational Series, Inc., 1998.

Athan, Mattie Sue and Deter, Dianalee. *The African Grey Parrot Handbook.* Hauppauge, NY: Barron's Educational Series, Inc., 2000.

Athan, Mattie Sue. *Guide to the Quaker Parrot.* Hauppauge, NY: Barron's Educational Series, Inc., 1997.

Athan, Mattie Sue and Deter, Dianalee. *The Second-hand Parrot.* Hauppauge, NY: Barron's Educational Series, Inc., 2002.

Lanterman, Werner. *Cockatoos.* Hauppauge, NY: Barron's Educational Series, Inc. 2000.

McElroy, Katy. *Eclectus Parrots.* Hauppauge, NY: Barron's Educational Series, Inc., 2002.

Wright, Maggie. *African Grey Parrots.* Hauppauge, NY: Barron's Educational Series, Inc., 2001.

Videos

"Fantastic Performing Parrots," Robar Productions, 1994.

"Parrots: Look Who's Talking," Thirteen/WNET and BBC-TV, 1995.

"Spirits of the Rainforest," Discovery Communications, Inc., 1993.

"Vanishing Birds of the Amazon," Audubon Productions and Turner Original Productions, 1996.

Web Sites

goodfeather.com: This site features general information on parrots, brief pieces on behavior, and "links to the best birds around."

positivelyparrots.com: This site contains useful information on parrot adoption, behavior, and grooming. Their motto is "Making life easier for parrots and their people."

quakerville.com: Dedicated entirely to the Quaker Parrot, this site contains links to health-care ideas, general information, and plenty of pictures and stories featuring Quakers.

Glossary

Abandonment: separation from the flock

Aggression: hostile nipping, biting, or chasing

Behavior:

  Self-rewarding: an activity that is enacted solely for the pleasure of doing it

  Sexual: self-rewarding breeding-related behavior

Bite: use of the parrot's beak in a manner intended to cause damage or injury

Bonding: the connection with another bird, a human, an object, or a location that a bird exhibits and defends

Call: a redundant, routine, or presumed-to-be natural vocalization

Covert: a layer of feathers that protect the bases and new growth of the wing's long feathers

DNA sexing: laboratory technique used to determine a parrot's gender

Down: the small, fuzzy feathers next to the body that are normally covered by contours

Droppings: the combination of urates, water, and fecal material excreted from the vent

Feather:

Chewing: self-inflicted feather damage to any part of the feather

Picking: any kind of self-inflicted feather damage

Plucking: pulling feathers from the follicles

Shredding: self-inflicted damage to the edge of the feathers

Snapping: self-inflicted feather damage to the center shaft

Feces: excreted solid waste, usually "worm-like" that can be differentiated from urates and liquid urine

Fight-or-flight response: instinctual, automatic reaction to real or perceived danger

Fledge: the process of a bird growing feathers and learning to fly

Flock: the basic social group of parrots

Forage: the process of seeking and consuming food

Habit: redundant behavior

Microchip: surgically implanted identification system

Mimic: to copy modeled behavior, especially vocalizations

Model: a learning process in which one individual copies behavior from another

Molt: the cyclical shedding and replacing of feathers

Neonate: a baby parrot that cannot yet sustain itself by eating food

Nipping: an accidental or non-aggressive pinch

Patterning: stimulating an individual to repeat behaviors through repetition

Pinning: the opening and closing of the iris that denotes excitement

Play: to engage in self-rewarding behaviors

Preen: to groom the feathers

Prey species: a species of animal typically sized and eaten by other animals

Roost: the place where a bird usually sleeps

Scream: loud, raucous call

Sexual maturity: the period during which breeding-related behaviors become prominent

Stress: any stimulus, especially fear or pain, that inhibits normal psychological, physical, or behavioral balance

Urates: nitrogenous wastes; the solid "white" part of a bird's excrement

Vent: the opening through which droppings are excreted

Some pets are highly compatible, some are not.

I N D E X

About the Author

Mattie Sue Athan has studied companion parrot behavior since 1978. Her areas of special interest are the development of behavior in companion parrots and the effect of environment on companion pet behavior. Her first book, *Guide to a Well-Behaved Parrot*, in its second edition, remains an industry standard. Mattie Sue also wrote *Guide to Companion Parrot Behavior, Guide to the Quaker Parrot*, and, with Dianalee Deter, *The Second-hand Parrot, The African Grey Parrot Handbook*, and *Guide to the Senegal Parrot and Its Family*.

Photo Credits

Mattie Sue Athan: pages 4, 5, 17 (bottom), 24, 29 (top), 36, 37, 40 (top), 44 (top), 45, 48 (top and bottom), 52 (bottom left), 61, 64 (bottom), 76, 77, and 84 (top right and bottom right); Joan Balzarini: pages 25, 28 (bottom), 29 (bottom), 56, 57, 60, and 84 (top left); Dianalee Deter: pages 8 (bottom left), 9 (top), 52 (top left), 69, and 84 (bottom left); Isabelle Francais: pages 65 (bottom) and 85 (top right); Susan Green: pages 2–3, 8 (top left, top right, and bottom right), 12, 13, 17 (top left and top right), 28 (top), 29 (top), 40 (bottom), 41 (top and bottom), 49 (bottom), 52 (top right), 53, 64 (top), 65 (top), 68, 72 (bottom), 73 (top), 88 and 89; Ron Moat: pages 33 (top), and 73 (bottom); Margaret Saldivar: pages 16 (top and bottom), 32 (top and bottom), 33 (bottom), 44 (bottom), 52 (bottom right), and 85 (top left); John and Lynne Vincent: pages 9 (bottom), 80, 81, 85 (bottom left and right), and 93; and B. Everett Webb: pages 20, 49 (top), and 72 (top).

Cover Photos

Joan Balzarini

Important Note

Poorly socialized or unhealthy parrots may be a danger to humans in the household. If you are bitten or scratched by your parrot, you should consult your physician immediately.

Escaped non-native species may represent an environmental threat in some places. Outdoor release or unrestricted outdoor flight is absolutely condemned by the ethical parrot keeper. This book recommends that a parrot's wing feathers be carefully trimmed at least three times yearly.

Dedication

Portia, the bird that started it all for me.

Acknowledgments

This book was fun for me because it represented reconnecting to those first days of living with parrots. I'd like to thank Dianalee Deter and Cathy Isbell, who were always there to help me find just the right words. Also, thanks to Dr. Paul Welch, Dr. Carol Best, Carl and Linda Moss, Pam Crookham, Liz Wilson, Rick Jordan, Sandee Molenda, and a generous assortment of other friends and dignitaries who provided suggestions and support. And none of this would have happened without the early contributions of Gale Whittington.

All inquiries should be addressed to:
Barron's Educational Series, Inc.
250 Wireless Boulevard
Hauppauge, NY 11788
http://www.barronseduc.com

Library of Congress Catalog Card No. 2002019815
International Standard Book No. 0-7641-2096-4

Library of Congress Cataloging-in-Publication Data
Athan, Mattie Sue.
　　Parrots: everything about purchase, care, feeding, and housing / Mattie Sue Athan; illustrations by Michele Earle-Bridges.
　　　　p. cm.
　　Includes bibliographical references (p.).
　　ISBN 0-7641-2096-4
　　1. Parrots. I. Title.

SF473.P33 A848 2002
636.6'865—dc21　　　　　　　　　2002019815

Printed in China
9 8 7 6 5 4 3